CONQUERING JERICHO

THE BIBLICAL GUIDE TO CRUSH MENTAL ILLNESS

Terrence A. Harris

Copyright © 2019 Terrence A. Harris.

All rights reserved. No part of this book may be used or reproduced by any means, graphic, electronic, or mechanical, including photocopying, recording, taping or by any information storage retrieval system without the written permission of the author except in the case of brief quotations embodied in critical articles and reviews.

This book is a work of non-fiction. Unless otherwise noted, the author and the publisher make no explicit guarantees as to the accuracy of the information contained in this book and in some cases, names of people and places have been altered to protect their privacy.

WestBow Press books may be ordered through booksellers or by contacting:

WestBow Press
A Division of Thomas Nelson & Zondervan
1663 Liberty Drive
Bloomington, IN 47403
www.westbowpress.com
1 (866) 928-1240

Because of the dynamic nature of the Internet, any web addresses or links contained in this book may have changed since publication and may no longer be valid. The views expressed in this work are solely those of the author and do not necessarily reflect the views of the publisher, and the publisher hereby disclaims any responsibility for them.

Any people depicted in stock imagery provided by Getty Images are models, and such images are being used for illustrative purposes only.
Certain stock imagery © Getty Images.

ISBN: 978-1-9736-5991-4 (sc)
ISBN: 978-1-9736-5993-8 (hc)
ISBN: 978-1-9736-5992-1 (e)

Library of Congress Control Number: 2019904228

Print information available on the last page.

WestBow Press rev. date: 04/24/2019

Scripture quotations marked (NLT) are taken from the Holy Bible, New Living Translation, copyright ©1996, 2004, 2015 by Tyndale House Foundation. Used by permission of Tyndale House Publishers, Inc., Carol Stream, Illinois 60188. All rights reserved.

Scripture quotations marked TPT are from The Passion Translation®. Copyright © 2017, 2018 by Passion & Fire Ministries, Inc. Used by permission. All rights reserved. ThePassionTranslation.com.

Scripture quotations taken from the New American Standard Bible® (NASB), Copyright © 1960, 1962, 1963, 1968, 1971, 1972, 1973, 1975, 1977, 1995 by The Lockman Foundation Used by permission. www.Lockman.org

Scripture taken from the King James Version of the Bible.

Scripture taken from the New King James Version®. Copyright © 1982 by Thomas Nelson. Used by permission. All rights reserved.

The Holy Bible, Berean Study Bible, BSB Copyright ©2016, 2018 by Bible Hub Used by Permission. All Rights Reserved Worldwide.

The Holy Bible, Berean Literal Bible, BLB Copyright ©2016, 2018 by Bible Hub Used by Permission. All Rights Reserved Worldwide.

Scripture quotations marked (NIV) are taken from the Holy Bible, New International Version®, NIV®. Copyright © 1973, 1978, 1984, 2011 by Biblica, Inc.™ Used by permission of Zondervan. All rights reserved worldwide. www.zondervan.com The "NIV" and "New International Version" are trademarks registered in the United States Patent and Trademark Office by Biblica, Inc.™

Scripture quotations marked MSG are taken from THE MESSAGE, copyright © 1993, 2002, 2018 by Eugene H. Peterson. Used by permission of NavPress. All rights reserved. Represented by Tyndale House Publishers, Inc.

Scripture quotations are from the ESV® Bible (The Holy Bible, English Standard Version®), copyright © 2001 by Crossway, a publishing ministry of Good News Publishers. Used by permission. All rights reserved.

Scripture quotations marked (AMP) are taken from the Amplified Bible, Copyright © 1954, 1958, 1962, 1964, 1965, 1987 by The Lockman Foundation. Used by permission.

Scripture quotations marked NLV are taken from the New Life Version, copyright © 1969 and 2003. Used by permission of Barbour Publishing, Inc., Uhrichsville, Ohio 44683. All rights reserved.

<u>Jesus Christ healed my mental illness.</u>

Sorry but not sorry. I just testify of His evidence,
Know this, men under the sun, the Son of Man's precedence,
I'm not here to offend, but neither am I here to pretend,
The chemical medicinal concoctions did pacify,
yet it was the Power and Wisdom of God,
who rectified.
So, I'm here to exhort you through,
To the One to Whom all praise is due,
To Him by His power, All Hell subdued,
Unlocked eternal chains, for His Word held truth.
Denied, said nye, He died but gave Rise,
And His Fire I did breathe, Now, I, Come Alive!
As We tread, defeat fails
The victory of Christ is certain
And He ensures beneath my feet
remains crushed
the head and purpose of the Serpent.

Terrence Harris

I came to you in weakness—timid and trembling. And my message and my preaching were very plain. Rather than using clever and persuasive speeches, I relied only on the power of the Holy Spirit. I did this so you would trust not in human wisdom but in the power of God.

1 Corinthians 2:3-5 NLT

Your Authority Granted

Jesus replied,

"While you were ministering, I watched Satan topple until he fell suddenly

From heaven like lightning to the ground...Now you understand that I have imparted to you All My authority to trample over his kingdom. You will trample upon every demon before you and overcome every power Satan possesses. Absolutely nothing will be able to harm you as you walk in this authority. However, your real source of joy isn't merely that these spirits submit to your authority, but that your names are written in the journals of heaven and that you belong to God's kingdom. This is the true source of your authority." Luke 10:18-20 TPT

By No Other Means And No Other Way

"And I will cause hostility between you and the woman, and between your offspring and her offspring. He will strike your head, and you will strike his heel.""

Genesis 3:15 NLT

Jesus Christ is the Seed who has been given the authority to crush the head of Satan and set us free from the power of darkness.

"You are from God, little children, and have overcome them; because greater is He who is in you than he who is in the world."

1 John 4:4 NASB

The power of Christ Jesus has overcome the power of Satan and every power from Hell. Nothing nor anyone else has this authority. "If Satan has risen up against himself and is divided, he cannot stand, but he is finished! But no one can enter the strong man's house and plunder his property unless he first binds the strong man, and then he will plunder his house." Jesus Christ - Mark 3:26-27 NASB Make no mistake nor underestimate the power and might of Satan... but the power of God our Savior Christ Jesus did and will bind the hands of the "strong man" over your life, plunder his house and bring us back to our Heavenly Father where we belong as well as everything we've lost.

"So, *if the Son sets you free, you are truly free.*" Jesus Christ - John 8:36 NLT. We tend to think and believe that all we need is a little drink, a little smoke, maybe a relationship, a long vacation to an exotic island, or more money, or more possessions in order to be set free from the struggles and cares in this life. But if the Son Jesus Christ is made Lord and Savior over your heart, mind and your life AND everything in it, your permanent parole and release from any spiritual prison has been granted. Anything, person or any vice in your life that has you chained and bound to self-destruction, Jesus promises that we are set free indeed.

"There is therefore now no condemnation to them which are in Christ Jesus, who walk not after the flesh, but after the Spirit."

Apostle Paul - Romans 8:1 KJV

The devil may tell you to cover up your guilt, shame, or stay busy so you don't have to think about your past. But we tend to "flee" from God because our sins and sin nature that is chained to us have been judged and they tremble at the thought of God's wrath. So, as they are attempting to escape judgment that is inevitable, they drag us away with them from the cross of Jesus Christ. But the cross, my friend, is for the breaking away of our chains from sin and its judgment thereof. We are made in the Father's image and therefore running towards God instead of away from Him is actually for our benefit, both in this life and for our eternal life to come. So, know that the Holy Spirit convicts us to move towards God's love and righteousness, while Satan condemns us to run or turn away from God. By either abhorring and hating God or falsely fearing His judgment, Satan desires that we who are created in God's image share the same destruction that was initially only meant for Satan and his angels, those who cast their lots with him to rebel against heaven. Jesus Christ our God, on the other hand, wants us to be residents of heaven.

"*He is the* STONE WHICH WAS REJECTED *by you,* THE BUILDERS, *but* WHICH BECAME THE CHIEFCORNER *stone. And there is salvation in no one else; for there is no other name under heaven that has been given among men by which we must be saved.*" Apostle

Peter - Acts 4:12 NASB. There isn't a healer, doctor, counselor, friend (sorry bros), brother, or advisor in this world or on earth that has the power and authority to save you and redeem your soul, especially from the oppression of mental illness, other than Jesus Christ. There is no healing and victory over mental illness, behavior health issues and the deep-rooted issues plaguing our hearts other than the love and power of Christ. And this renewal and purification of our heart and soul starts with us bringing ourselves to humility and repenting of our sins, (God knows how many) and the receiving of Jesus Christ into our hearts as Lord and Savior over our entire lives. We then must ask Christ to show us His ways and to empower us to walk in them while also asking for the strength, love and a willing heart to forgive those who've caused us pain and heal all of the hurt in our life as well. And by the power of God's Holy Spirit who will be with us, to lead us all the days of our life into eternal life in heaven with Christ Jesus and our Heavenly Father forever and ever. Amen.

If I do not make it crystal clear that apart from the power and love of Jesus Christ, that I am nothing and I could do nothing, especially while in the chains of mental illness,

...then I have written this book in vain.

The Reason and Call For Acceptance

"...for dust you are and to dust you will return."

After the Fall of Man, excerpt of Genesis 3:19 NIV

"When Adam sinned, sin entered the world.

Adam's sin brought death, so, death spread to everyone, for everyone sinned." Romans 5:12 NLT

"For the wages of sin is death; but the gift of God is eternal life through Jesus Christ our Lord." Romans 6:23 KJV

    The world is not just sick and unbalanced, every created being and thing in it, when arriving here, is rotated into the process of decay and then of Death, hopefully for all, just once, yet for many, twice...and these consequences of Adam's invitation to sin, since that time, has never played fair.
    It shows no favoritism.

Ecclesiastes 9:2 BSB says, "It is the same for all: There is a common fate for the righteous and the wicked, for the good and the bad, for the clean and the unclean, for the one who sacrifices and the one who does not. As it is for the good, so it is for the sinner; as it is for the one who makes a vow, so it is for the one who refuses to take a vow."

Death comes to all. Can you imagine being Adam and living for 930 years and how he may have felt at year 400? Some of us feel like it's almost over at 40 years old! Adam and Eve gave birth to Seth when Adam was 130 years old so it could be said that because of the effects of sin, Adam died or decayed for at least 800 years. That is being alive to witness not only the slow decay of his own body, soul and spirit but of his family and the earth... for eight generations. We were originally not born to die but rather, because of the entering of sin, born into death, but we were created by God, The Creator, to be alive. And this Earth was designed to be an extension of...as It Is in Heaven. Yet when Man received the two cents of disobedience, it was an exchange that went spiritually and eternally wrong. So, we are now living in a world that is dying, and more so, where mental illness is just one component of sin's decaying agent.

Acceptance.

"Those who use the things of the world should not become attached to them. For this world as we know it will soon pass away."

1 Corinthians 7:31 NLT

A beginning step to healing is to come to the agreement with the Word of The Lord: The world and everything in it is perishing. It is not getting better.

But a perishing world is not the end of all things that exist.
For the love and faithfulness of God *is not* perishing. It never will.

So, in order to "live" and be truly *alive* in a world that is dying, the focus then becomes to be saved by the love of God through the faith in the resurrection of His son Jesus Christ, who leads us to eternal life. Then, to a world that is dying, inquire of the Lord God to be His agent in His work for His glory, in the snatching of those out of the same hell fire through the power of Christ Jesus that was once, before Christ, consuming our souls. This decision brings us to life in a lifeless world: being a part of the redeeming work of God, for the love of God desires that none perish but receive eternal life. It's apparent that it is actually becoming more of a necessity for the world to have than tons of wealth and possessions. As the world grows dim, things such as love, peace, wisdom, honesty and truth, understanding, purpose, healing, joy, restoration, provisions and needs being fulfilled, are as valuable as or more so than clean water. Yet, all of these belong to and come from the Living God. The Light of God is rearing through the darkness to show us the way to conqueror our Jericho, to reach victory over our battles and against a deep and Godly-abhorred foundation in our personal lives, in which, apart from Christ has become a mighty stronghold. But by the power of God's Holy Spirit and obedience to His Word, while believing that He cannot fail, Christ descends below any foundation and stronghold opposed to His victory - and He utterly tears it down. Knowing that everyone and everything else has failed to restore our minds, there is a way to win this battle. For since the power of sin has been arrested by God through Christ Jesus, then the power of mental illness has been arrested as well. AND by the same power of God, you have been offered the gift and power,

To not just deal with it.

Not just manage it.

Not just suppress it.

But be Victorious over it.

And Conquer it.

Release Me. Now!

What are Mental Illnesses and Behavioral Health Problems exactly?

We've heard that mental illness is a health condition where a person's thinking, mood and behavior is affected by different life circumstances such as stress and problems in family life, work, etc. Behavior Health Issues stem from actions such as substance abuse that turn into addictions. But one, the latter, is or can be influenced by the weighing effects of the former.

Deeper cause.

Stressful Job. Traumatic experience. Genetics. Environment. Lifestyle. That's pretty good. But deeper meaning please. Knowledge and expertise of mental illness and behavior health issues, after evaluating different definitions, stops here.

After determining the causes of this "disease", the conversation then moves to treatment and medicinal options available. Ok…but what about the cure of it? For it to be conquered and done away with forever?

The answer: In order to "conquer" mental illness we first must understand that it is a subcategory of consequences related to a main issue plaguing our society – sin.

"Bible God talk?" Me: Yes.

"Jesus Preachy Freak talk?" Me: Yep.

Short testimony: I had and was diagnosed with mental illness…before. In 2010-2011, I was back and forth in the hospital. During this time, I was admitted to a couple of mental health institutions for a significant amount of time. I have taken psychotic medication such as Zyprexa, Risperidone, and another anti-anxiety medication I can't think of name right now, I think Buspar. I've wandered around outside, I've felt like death was around the corner every single day, so I didn't sleep because I was afraid to. And when I did sleep, 6-8 hours felt like 30 minutes, so I was exhausted. Depression. No motivation in life. I suffered from panic attacks often (I could actually feel them coming on) and acute psychosis episodes. I couldn't eat. I hated seeing the sunlight in the morning and the nighttime was eerie and I could hear all kinds of sounds including my heart beat.

...And I have now been released from the necessity of taking psychotic medication and from the power of mental illness through the power of God in Christ Jesus. And since I was and am released from its power, I desire the same for you. I wish this on no one. Not even my enemies (if I have them). Most importantly, God desires for you to be released, healed, and empowered through the Holy Spirit and a conqueror of mental illness. So here are your options: You can both be released and freed from this "prison" and given authority over it and subdue it or you can spend the rest of your life, wrestling with it, treating or better yet "masking" the symptoms and causes with drugs and physical "remedies". Take your pick. But whatever you choose, the foundation and root cause of the topic of discussion is nothing to play with. It's destructive to life and can and will do the same to you. The truth of the matter is that, though medical treatment has some physical benefits and, in some cases, should not be discredited but considered, the root cause and concerns of "mental illness" derive from the conditions of a person's soul and the spirit that is guiding or leading them. And these conditions enter through and are now "realized" by the body or the better term: our flesh. And the vice of our flesh – once again, sin.

Therefore, since the wages of sin is death, we then know that the precursor of all death is all disease.

> *nósos – a chronic (persisting) disease, typically an incurable ailment. In other words, it is a terminal disease to where there is no natural cure.*

In the days of Christ Jesus, according to scripture, these kinds of diseases were known to be demon-imposed sicknesses. The demon-possessed man confronted and healed by Jesus Christ at the burial caves in Mark 5: 1-20 (NASB) could not be cured naturally. The conversation Jesus had with the man is clearly showing that the "legion" of evil spirits had complete control over his actions and speech - so the only counselor that could have truly reached down into the foundation of the demon- possessed man's situation is the Wonderful Counselor Jesus Christ. Other than that, like psychiatric medication, trying to chain him up to restrain him was like placing a natural band- aid on an area of the body that has received severe blunt-force trauma.

Therefore "mental illness" in a nutshell is actually *spiritual oppression and opposition.*

We know or have heard that human beings consist of having a Mind, Body, and Soul. We've also heard it as Body, Soul, and Spirit. The problem is that when a soul is oppressed by an evil spirit such as a lying spirit (verbal abuse, gossip, hearing and believing false knowledge and wisdom of one's self, perceived fears), a violent spirit (rape, abuse, molestation, physical abuse and altercations) sexually/immoral spirits (lust, carousing, pornography, fornication, sex outside of God's will of marriage, adultery) which then festers and invites other evil spirits that introduce other doctrines that is in opposition to God and His word. Anger, drunkenness, witchcraft (the use of drugs for the sake of getting "high" and escaping - we will talk about this in a later chapter) murder, rage, pride, cowardice, self-degradation and esteem issues, lack of self-worth even thoughts leading to suicide. The problem is where we believe that our medicinal and physical efforts, like pills and exercise, alone can solve these issues, when in fact, beneath the underlying surfaces, they are literally demonic onslaughts. Some are also rather chastening and can be devastating. The medicinal approach to solving mental illness apart from Christ Jesus is similar to installing thousands of 12-feet-tall-white-picket-fences back to back in a row...directly in front of a moving enemy tank that's headed towards your home base. I know that's some visual but that's how I see it. The tall white fences prevent you from seeing the tank, in a way to "convince" you to forget about it because you don't see it, which is also known as masking the tank with a resolution that is highly temporary, costly and not fully reliable. But Christ Jesus brings the land mines, anti-tank rockets, and warfare from the friendly skies, heaven that is, in which you can call in for support whenever you need. For the Word of God goes deeper to the roots and foundation of every human need, problem, issue and oppression than any angel, demon or person can go. God's Word is mighty to heal and restore and He is mighty to tear down and destroy enemy vices and fortresses. If Jesus Christ can release (and He did) the captives of old and ancient times of Sheol after the Savior's death on the cross at Calvary, then releasing you and I from our captivities while we walk on the face of this Earth is no biggie to Him. The words of Christ Jesus have both healed and subdued the oppression and possession by Satan and every demonic force on people and Christ Jesus also has the authority to call thousands upon thousands of war angels to His side. And the good news is this: when Christ Jesus dwells richly in our hearts through the power of the Holy Spirit, this authority and victory over the world has been and is abundantly supplied to you. This biblical passage addresses the knowledge of "mental illness" in the days Jesus walked the earth and the only answer to it. This is the power of our Savior Jesus- Mark 5:1-20 NLT: *So, they arrived at the other side of the lake, in the region of the Gerasenes. When Jesus climbed out of the boat, a man possessed by an evil spirit came out from the tombs to meet him. This man lived in the burial caves and could no longer be restrained, even with a chain. Whenever he was put into chains and shackles— as he often was—he snapped the chains from his wrists and smashed the shackles. No one was strong enough to subdue him. Day and night, he wandered among the burial caves and in the hills, howling and cutting himself with sharp stones. When Jesus was still some distance away, the man saw him, ran to meet him, and bowed low before him. With a shriek, he screamed, "Why are you interfering with me, Jesus, Son of the Most High God? In the name of God, I beg you, don't torture me!" For Jesus had already said to the spirit, "Come out of the man, you evil spirit." Then Jesus demanded, "What is your name?" And he replied, "My name is Legion, because there are many of us inside this man." Then the evil spirits begged him again and again not to send them to some distant place. There happened to be a large herd of pigs feeding on the hillside nearby. "Send us into those pigs," the spirits begged. "Let us enter them." So, Jesus gave them permission. The evil spirits came out of the man and entered the pigs, and the entire herd of about 2,000 pigs plunged down the steep hillside into the lake and drowned in the water.*

There are some things that stood out in the verses to me regarding the spirits possessing the man: The man "conscientiously" lived in the tombs. Why? Isolation from Light and isolation or "rejection" of those created in God's imagine. Demons carry the same manner. Swine are some of the nastiest animals there could ever be, being that they are ok with eating their own feces, and washing and wallowing in it, yet the swine didn't even want to be associated with these spirits possessing the man but chose to rather run off the cliff to their death– that's how horrible evil spirits are. A person dealing with mental health issues can sometimes be unpredictable. I know from first- hand experience what it feels like to be restrained. One day I had thought I could escape the facility, so as the facility doors that the doctors and workers walked through had opened from one section of the facility to the next I went for it and ran as fast as I could and then tried to jump kick a door down that proved to be quite secure and I then was met by about four to five "restrainers" who pinned me down and clowned me for thinking I could escape that way. But there were so many restrainers on me because a person in this state of mind or spirit at this point isn't thinking about their body and the consequences; they are all mind and spirit- and this mind or spirit can be extremely overpowering. So, concerning the man at the caves, no doubt in my mind in my personal knowledge, along with the testimony that fallen angels or demons being very real, the man with a legion of them would have not been restrained by those chains. People struggling with mental and behavioral health issues find it difficult to sleep at night. So, they need sedatives whether prescribed or self-medicated to relax their mind so they can rest – but as we know they wear off by or before the end of the day. Obscure "communication" and actions, especially amongst one's self such "howling" in this man's case or "yelling and arguing at no one" or sometimes a person is "mentally not present." Sharp stones have been replaced with razor blades, cigarette burns, dermatillomania, drug abuse and needles to numb the internal pain by inflicting physical pain on the body, so the mind doesn't focus on the internal pain. But most importantly these evil spirits are powerless against and at the mercy of the Man and Savior Christ Jesus. Physical harm to one's self, depression, paranoias and anxieties, abnormal psychotic emotions and behaviors, thoughts and verbal expressions of suicide or harm to others is not from God. And God loves you too much to be a God of punishment and suffering, for He is the God of love and restoration. As we spend time knowing God also as our Counselor in life and spend time with other godly people who can speak healing and power into to our life, through fellowship, we will grow stronger and once again have a purity and peace in our mind. This is a powerful testimony for this man to have, and from this point on, the Lord will empower you through the Holy Spirit to speak victory into the life of your neighbors and friends around you.

Who Am I?

It's a question that everyone has asked themselves either once or a thousand times or more, realizing that the place that they are in life, whether at a lifeless job, a broken or difficult relationship, or a long, dragged out season of trials, is nowhere near identical to the amazing dreams and desires that God has placed in our hearts. So, we keep up with the daily triangle of death where we go to work, come home, go to bed, wake up and go to work, come home and go to bed, and we repeat this cycle hoping to finally answer the question in the midst of our daily routine, "Who am I and what am I doing here?" I remember being an employee at a Fortune 100 Company and while there I put all of my eggs in this basket and faith in the idea that since I was a creative person with ideas, and their niche revolved around design, show and innovation, it only made sense to me to proclaim this: I am an aspiring creative designer for Fortune 100 Company. Well, I applied to intern for the Creative Department and other departments at the company for 11 years, to no avail. When you don't even qualify to work for FREE at an establishment doing what you are passionate about doing, it makes one question his or her purpose or focus. Then I thought, maybe I should direct my thoughts to a different profession or career or just maybe I'm not that good creatively to begin with. While working for the company, I didn't feel a strong passion in any other area, nor did I aspire to work longer term for the department I was working in for that matter. But the keep-on- trying "exhortations" from others and the "this is a great company to work for" spiel, in addition the "comfortable and secure" job with decent benefits can cause a person to voluntarily conform and settle for who their job title says they are. And it wore into me and led me to an atmosphere of uncertainty with no perceived purpose and eventually depression, a lack of motivation, stress and anxiety with panic attacks and then a mental ward (or two) after breaking down. This wasn't the only thing that was going on with me at the time, but it added fuel to the fire.

The Holy Spirit gave me this scripture to jot down as I'm writing this chapter:

Matthew 4:18-22 NIV:

> As Jesus was walking beside the Sea of Galilee, he saw two brothers, Simon called Peter and his brother Andrew. They were casting a net into the lake, for they were fishermen. "Come, follow me," Jesus said, "and I will send you out to fish for people." At once they left their nets and followed him. Going on from there, he saw two other brothers, James son of Zebedee and his brother John. They were in a boat with their father Zebedee, preparing their nets. Jesus called them, and immediately they left the boat and their father and followed him.

You know what I think why they didn't ask Jesus where they were going and "At once left their nets" and again, "immediately they left the boat and their father?" Because Peter and Andrew hated their job title. You can't convince me that they didn't. The boat James and John were on wasn't a cruise ship or anything special and probably wasn't going much further than the eye could see. I guarantee that it was because the idea of "just being a fisherman" or "just being a net preparer...." and in my case, just being an employee is, for a lack of better words, for the birds, especially when God created you for more. Much more than you can imagine. It wasn't enough for James and John to "just be the sons of their earthly fisherman father", to no offense of course to the great dad's out here. The beautiful thing of that passage lies a strong truth to this day: every great dad wants or should want their child or children to grow up and be better than themselves. They left their nets to follow Christ and that was the last we heard of anything concerning their father in the fishing boat. We don't just want to breathe, we want to come alive and come to life! We need this. It has to be more to life than just this (as I'd gesture to everything in my immediate surroundings).

It has to be more than working a regular 9-5, struggling to make ends meet. There has to be more to life than to just get rich and have all the possessions money can buy. You can grind to make one million dollars, then when you get it, how ironic the soul can be that it's no longer satisfied until it makes two million dollars. From there, three million, then four million. Then you ask yourself, "Why am I still not happy?" "Why do I feel something is missing even though I have everything the world says you need to be happy?" There has to be more that believing that the acquisition of "things and people" will be the source of my joy and happiness, only to find out that people are simply, well, people. At the end of the day, our purpose is still not clear. There has to be more to life than all of the corruption of the world: We want to help those in need but we don't know how to help effectively, because there are some who really need a helping hand to move forward and some, let's just be honest, just want a hand out, are capable of working hard but just don't want to because they can constantly get what they need for free. Then we sometimes give cautiously in fear of our giving not reaching who it needs to reach because of possible scams. It seems like a lot of the stories reported in the news are either depressing, shared to subconsciously instill fear and negativity in society for the sakes of creating a "wow" factor and growing viewer ratings, as well as introducing prejudices and excessive stereotypes instead of creating unity and community.

What should we do? What shouldn't we do? Who can we trust? Who can't we trust?

Yep. Sometimes even our feelings towards people. They now become, "What is this?" There has to be more.

I imagine what Peter and Andrew thought when Jesus said He was going to teach them to fish for people. If I was with them, I would have looked at the water and thought, "it's people down there, fam'?" "Well, whatever. Teach me what I need to know and lead me to where I need to go because anything is better than this." And if Jesus Christ was going to be the only One to truly usher me into the eternal and abundant life in all things, and I mean *real living*, then Jesus I belong to You, sign me up and let's do this.

It was in the midst of the mental illness, depression, anxiety and my brokenness when I made a conscious decision to truly follow Christ Jesus as my Lord and Savior before I lost my mind; there was no more playing church for me. God then put His seal on me and His Spirit in me and called me His own. Eternal Life was breathed into me and He nurtured me back to health and I began to see that I was created by my Heavenly Father as His masterpiece and with a purpose; for much more than my hourly position at "Fortune 100 Company". From that point on, I was no longer defined by my past sins, my failures or successes, or a job title, not by the quantity or quality of my possessions or by my personal aspirations in the world, nor even by the name given to me by my parents. Rather, I am now called by Him, to Whom I belong, a child of the Righteous King, and a slave for the sake of Christ Jesus to operate in this world in any way my Heavenly Father wills, calls and empowers me to operate. I AM who *He* says I am... Absolutely not by social media and the Internet unless what you hear is inspired by the Bible–The Word of God. Absolutely not by popular culture, television, movies, and music unless these are inspired by the Word of God. Absolutely not by the stereotypes and prejudices of this fallen world and society has rooted in themselves concerning you or anyone else. Not even by your best friend unless they are telling you what God's Holy Word says about you.

Who Does I AM Say You Are?

I AM... the name of God. It was given to Himself by Himself when speaking to Moses while in the bonds of Egypt.

> Moses said to God, "Suppose I go to the Israelites and say to them, 'The God of your fathers has sent me to you,' and they ask me, 'What is his name?' Then what shall I tell them?" God said to Moses, "I AM WHO I AM. This is what you are to say to the Israelites: 'I AM has sent me to you.'" Exodus 3:13, 14 NLT

So, the title of the chapter and question is rather this:
Who does The Creator of Heaven and Earth say you are? Who are YOU according to HIS WORD?

Not by the word of your mother or father or siblings.

Not by your occupation or career.

Not by your circumstance or experiences.

Not by your spouse or children.

Not by all the money and possessions you have (or do not have).

Definitely not by your enemy...unless you're an enemy of God.

Nor by your best friend unless they are telling you what God says about you.

Despite the things people, or even you yourself, have spoken and believed about yourself, despite the rumors that people have said to you or behind your back or despite the things you've done to others, how does God see you? Who is *He* calling and growing *you* to be? And who and what is

He *not* calling you to be? It is important to know that when it's all said and done, the only viewpoint and word that holds "fullness" and is without void is what God has spoken concerning you by His Word.

> You are loved by the God, the Creator of the Universe.

> Yet you, in truth, though you were created *good*, were indeed born sinful…But still, you are valued. You are wanted.

> You are loved by the Father. You *are* indeed known…for He knows you intimately well. You behold His likeness.

> You are NEVER alone. God's got your back.

> You bring joy to God's heart because you are His masterpiece and prize creation. You have a purpose in this life.

> No, you are NOT a mistake. You are mighty, with Christ Jesus.

> You will overcome ANYTHING through the power of Jesus Christ. You are rich.

> Your Heavenly Father has all that you need in His Kingdom to live an abundant life, first spiritually and also physically, while on Earth, in which you have this inheritance… through Christ Jesus.

> You are forgiven, but only He is the gift of forgiveness that you must receive.

The world today would have called the Prophet Moses, King David and the Apostle Paul murderers who are only good for wrath and condemnation. Fear of punishment, death and hopelessness was high on my list when it came to my past fears, stressors, paranoias and depression. But despite their faults, God called these men patriarchs and Men of God, each in their flawed past as violators of God's Law, to lead God's children towards the Promise and to tell the world who He is. Therefore, even if I have a flawed past as well, Jesus will also qualify me "called" according to His eternal mercies and grace upon the cross. Yet we, upon receiving this gift and answering His calling for our lives, are then called by Him, chosen. And when *chosen* by the Lord: *Armed*. Moses led the Children of Israel to the physical "Promised Land" (Israel) on earth from Egypt, in which was at that time the physical place of the Hebrew's bondage. King David held the Savior of the world, Christ Jesus, the Promise of Redemption and Salvation, in his loins, though he too violated God's Law. Apostle Paul, a destroyer of Christians, was called by Christ to nurture and build God's children through Christ, and also those who were called to receive and know fully the Promise and Gift years to come. As we come to the cross and believe that the cross was for the covering and propitiation for our sins; that when Christ died on the cross and then three days later He rose from the dead by the power of God through the Holy Spirit, we too, through the power of the Holy Spirit can be and have been given the true gift to be resurrected spiritually and given New Life and a righteous standing with God. Freed from the bondage of death in our sin nature and the fears it releases and anxieties that torment the whole world, we have now received and are receiving love and power to follow God and have a life pleasing to Him, and to be in right standing with Him, leading us to eternal life. It was never God's will for Man to suffer the way that he is, but the disobedience and sin committed from the beginning in the flesh and body of Adam was then transferred to all men, generation after generation after generation causing all to degenerate both physically and most importantly and unfortunately, spiritually. For the wages of sin is death. But Jesus Christ bore this punishment and has freed us to now be whom God, our Heavenly Father, has called and created us to be and to resemble Him, whom we were called to resemble from the beginning of time. In all of the guilt that you're feeling and the pain that you suffered in your personal life, we are to line it up with the truth of God's Word and use it to cut down the lies of the enemy concerning ourselves, over. And over. And over again until the enemy flees from us. For when Satan attacks us, he flees only because we stand on God's truth and that we stand in Christ Jesus. We MUST know God's truth! Let us come before the throne and see who the Creator of

Heaven and earth, the ONLY One who breathed life into us and Who knew us before we were born, declare to us who we are. Only His eyes are perfect. Let's ask God to help us see ourselves the way He sees us.

Psalm 139:14 KJV says this, "I will praise Thee, for I am fearfully and wonderfully made: marvelous are thy works; and that my soul knoweth right well. Another version of the passage word says, "thank you for making me wonderfully complex your workmanship is marvelous!" When God created you, He didn't make any mistakes. He made you marvelous and it's time that you let go any word that does not line up with this truth.

The next scripture is Galatians 2:20 NIV, and it says this,

> *"I have been crucified with Christ and I no longer live but Christ lives in me. The life I now live in the body, I live by faith in the son of God, who loved me and gave himself for me. I do not set aside the grace of God, for if righteousness could be gained through the law, Christ died for nothing"*

So, only because of the Holy Spirit living inside of us, through faith in Jesus Christ, are we made righteous in the eyes of God. That's whose *truth*, not opinion, matters the most. That's what *He* calls us. Because when *He* sees us in Christ Jesus, He doesn't see our past failures, brokenness and mistakes. He sees the covering of His Son. The Father and Creator of the universe sees *His* creation aspiring and desiring to be more and more like His Son, who in truth, is well pleasing to the Father. And if we are in the Son and continue to follow Him, then we are well pleasing to our Heavenly Father as well.

There's a thing that's called generational curses, where the presumption is "Like father, like son". Whoever your earthly father is or was, the son is expected to follow suit in occupation, but most times they follow in character, behavior and habits. Yet the Heavenly Father is greater than earthly parents and He can adopt us and give us the power and freedom to imitate His Son. In my case, I had two, my biological father and my dad. The first time I met my biological father was in 2011, when I was 30 years old. We've connected on a few occasions and I've had no resentment nor did I ask, "Where were you all my life?" It wasn't awkward the first time we met, but kind of interesting and funny how much we look alike (Yea, he's the reason why my hair won't grow back and why I had to surrender to "the bald head.") Now, my late dad, who I was named after, was a no-nonsense, authority enforcer, which is needed when dealing with boys-especially in this day and age. He was a very good financial provider having a great job at Ford Motor Company. Yet there was a side to him that was kind of "flashy", a big talker and wanted to still live the life opposed to settling down fully with my mother. I was caught in the middle of his life style, where I was warned at a young age that if I told my mother about all of the "carousing" that he was involved in that he would punish me. There were times where he would pick me up pretending to spend time with me in front of my mother, only to drop me off at one of his female friend's house so he could go hang out with another woman or whatever he used to do. He would pick me back up and of course while being warned that I should conceal the fact that my father and I didn't even spend time together. I remember visiting my grandmother (his mother) in Greensboro, Alabama one summer. She, along with some of the family, knowing that he was supposed to be in a "common-law" marriage with my mother, freely welcomed him to invite other women over while he was visiting. He was a player. His motto was, "get as much sex as you can before you die." As I grew up, I began to withdraw psychologically from him because our personalities didn't mesh well from the beginning. But the seed of influence was planted in me. There came a time when we weren't even on speaking terms in a sense that I moved on to other priorities like trying to figure out who I was as a person or what I was going to do with my life for that matter. Things did change for us relationally for the better though, I believe it came at the announcement of him becoming ill, being diagnosed with heart failure and him knowing that he didn't have much time left to live. I had the opportunity to share some things on my heart with him while healing in my season of mental illness. I also had an opportunity to share with him that I dedicated my life to God in Christ. He also had the opportunity to hear my heart and apologize to me for things he's done wrong, we told each other we loved and missed each other thankfully before he passed away in 2013. He died without knowing his biological father, yet while searching for him he learned that his own father had passed a year previous to the beginning of his search for him. That had to hurt my dad deeply. He wasn't able to release his pain, share his frustrations in life and pains with the man who was supposed to be there for him from day one. He felt he had to substitute letting go, forgiveness and peace through Christ in exchange for alcohol and carousing to numb the pain. But I did learn from my dad, however, the concept of adoption - being claimed as my dad's own even when I wasn't truly by blood. I'm thankful though, that I've been adopted by the Father through our Savior Jesus Christ. I no longer had to be bound in my heart and mind with the generational curses and chains of my earthly fathers. I'm married now with a family of my own and God has blessed me with them and for them I am truly thankful. As a new family man, I am learning to set my heart to follow Christ Jesus in marriage and how to cut away the generational dross from the future generations that the Lord will allow to proceed from me. I now have the authority to be the man that God the Father is calling and has always called me to be. In no way is this "shade" on both of my earthly dad's, but it is what it is. I'm just thankful that God gave us the power and the freedom to imitate our Savior and to live life His way. I wish my dad could have known that God would have been the Heavenly Father that he's always needed and searched for on a personal and intimate level. As soon as I discovered 1 Kings 2:1-3 NASB, I cherished it as a passage of scripture. Even though the dialogue is between King David and his son Solomon, this was the beginning instruction to me on being a "real" father and a man in life.

"As David's time to die drew near, he charged Solomon his son, saying, "I am going the way of all the earth. Be strong, therefore, and *show yourself a man.*"

How dad?

"Keep the charge of the LORD your God, to walk in His ways, to keep His statutes, His commandments, His ordinances, and His testimonies, according to what is written in the Law of Moses, that you may succeed in all that you do and wherever you turn."

Done. (In progress for life)

I can exhort myself in knowing that as I abide in the Word of God and make His word the supreme and practical authority of every area and direction in my life, then I am strong. I AM a real man.

Now here's an additional blessing for all of us to know concerning our stance with our Heavenly Father through Christ Jesus.

Psalms 103: 8-18 MSG

GOD makes everything come out right; he puts victims back on their feet. He showed Moses how he went about his work, opened up his plans to all Israel. GOD is sheer mercy and grace; not easily angered, he's rich in love. He doesn't endlessly nag and scold, nor hold grudges forever. He doesn't treat us as our sins deserve, nor pay us back in full for our wrongs. As high as heaven is over the earth, so strong is his love to those who fear him. And as far as sunrise is from sunset, he has separated us from our sins. As parents feel for their children, GOD feels for those who fear him. He knows us inside and out, keeps in mind that we're made of mud. Men and women don't live very long; like wildflowers they spring up and blossom, but a storm snuffs them out just as quickly, leaving nothing to show they were here. GOD's love, though, is ever and always, eternally present to all who fear him, making everything right for them and their children as they follow his Covenant ways and remember to do whatever he said. Our sinful consciences have led us to believe that God has set His heart to punish us. But condemnation comes from and belongs to the devil and the wisdom and knowledge the world offers is that of demons. Take off this guilty conscious through faith in Christ Jesus, for He has given us the power through the Holy Spirit to break the chains of a guilty conscious and places our heart and mind in right standing with God.

My prayer is that you add these to your journal and spiritual arsenal whenever the thoughts creep in. You are valued and loved, God is with you in every area of your life, you have a purpose for living, and if you don't know who you are or who you belong to, God says," You can belong to Me." "But sit with Me and meditate on My Scriptures and become intimate with

My heart as it overflows through My Word concerning you." Receive them. Believe and walk inside the New Jericho, The Promise.

See these:

Exodus 6:7 NLT, God says this, "I will claim you as My own people and I will be your God. Then you will know that I am the Lord Your God Who has freed you from your oppression in Egypt."

Jeremiah 30:22 ESV, "And you shall be my people and I will be your God."

Isaiah 41:10 KJV, "so do not fear, for I am with you; Do not be dismayed, for I am your God. I will strengthen you and help you; I will uphold you with my righteous right hand."

Zephaniah 3:17 KJV God says this, For the LORD your God is living among you. He is a mighty savior. He will take delight in you with gladness. With his love, he will calm all your fears. He will rejoice over you with joyful songs."

Going through the healing process of mental illness is a long journey but as you meditate on the words in this passage as well as many others, we can understand God's heart in knowing that he is rooting for us and leading us towards the victorious heart and mind.

Romans 8:35-37 KJV, says this, "who shall separate us from the love of Christ? Shall trouble or hardship or persecution or famine or nakedness or danger or sword? As it is written: "For your sake we faced death all day long; we are considered sheep to be slaughtered. "No, in all these things we are more than conquerors through Him who loved us."

Call It As It Is

Let's just say...

You're tempted to think and feel like you're the worst of all people, having a guilty-ridden conscience for (fill in the blank_____.) You brand yourself as worthless and believe you will be nothing more than that because of the sexual, psychological and/or physical abuse you've experienced from someone who was supposed to love and protect you. You came from a home where your father or mother could have cared less about you. You are full of regret from the poor decisions you've made in the past where the consequences of those actions have painfully manifested themselves in some way in your life. You believe you are filthy because you believe what the thoughts and voices say about you and your past...

...And you, in both your thoughts and by others, are ridiculed and mocked for thinking that a Holy God would forgive *an unholy you*, wash *you* clean with His "Son's" blood, love *you*, set *you* free and then use *you* for serving Him in His Kingdom - to work *against* a kingdom you are now in bondage to?!

Reply: Yep...For it is written, "He who conceals his transgressions will not prosper, but he who confesses and forsakes them will find compassion." *Proverbs 28:13 NASB*

(...and the Lord wants His creation to prosper and wants to show compassion to the lost...)

Reply: Yep...For it is written, "If we confess our sins, He is faithful and just to forgive us our sins and to cleanse us from all unrighteousness." *1 John 1:9 BSB*

Reply: Pretty much...For it is written, (that King David said to the Lord) "I acknowledged my sin to You, and my iniquity I did not hide; I said, "I will confess my transgressions to the LORD"; And You forgave the guilt of my sin. Selah. *Psalm 32:5 NASB*

Reply: Kind of... For it is written the Lord said, "Come now, and let us reason together," Says the LORD, "Though your sins are as scarlet, they will be as white as snow; Though they are red like crimson, they will be like wool. *Isaiah 1:18 NASB*

Reply: In a nutshell for it is written, well... in all of Psalm 103 AMPV of David – but if you're preferable to another version then that will work as well.

Fighting with the Word of God is fighting with the Word of God.

For when the devil brings an accusation against you, let God and His Living Word fight for you and bring you victory and His joy. Do not listen to anything the devil has to say concerning being hopeless because of your sins, and definitely do not accept any condemnation and guilty he has to offer. Know that the enemy of our souls is looking to drag you to hell along with him and his angels. In the current day in age there is the thought that you are the god of your own life so do what thy will (do whatever you want to do and whatever makes you feel good).There is also the thought that sin doesn't exist and everybody is good, that we are nothing more than beasts and come from monkeys and do not possess a soul. Even to disbelieve in the existence of a God, Jesus Christ, a Creator of mankind is applauded by the world. The thought of a heaven for the good people and a hell for the bad people or a Satan (which is the thought pattern that Satan would prefer you have- because if he exists then why not God?) is obscure to most and therefore not taken as seriously. I remember people joking about the idea of going to hell with certain remarks as, "Heaven sounds boring. I want to go where the party is," The world may or may not believe in sin or the Lord God, but there can be no argument whatsoever that despair, decay, violence and vengeance, greed, envy and jealousy, anger and murder, suicide, sexual immoralities and lewdness, pride and selfishness and dying, all of which are precursors of death, is all around us on a daily basis.

The truth is this: that these *fruits* that we can witness at every turn are the results of sin being active in this world. Understand the word of God: "For the wages of sin is death, but the gift of God is eternal life in Christ Jesus our Lord." *(Romans 6:23 BSB)* Also, remember the scripture, Ephesians 4:27 ESV says, *"and give no opportunity to the devil or give the devil a foothold."* With every opportunity, the devil uses it to snatch you, my friend, from eternal life that Christ is offering. Don't give him an inch of any section of your life. Every morning that the Lord blesses you to wake up and see the day that He has made, start it off by thanking Him and asking Him to cover you with the blood of the Lamb and the full armor of God. Our daily prayers last for that long-24 hours. Let me also let you in on a little secret: With Jesus Christ as your Lord and Savior, eternal life will begin for you right at this very moment! This is one of the things that Jesus means and wants us to understand when He says that the Kingdom of God is at hand. The presence of God is now in your *actual* reach and accessible to those who receive Christ and desire to know the culture of Heaven *more*. You don't have to wait until you leave this earth in God to receive power, authority and victory over the devil and the renewal of yourself. The process of becoming sanctified in Jesus can begin today. For Jesus Christ said, "But you will receive power *when* the Holy Spirit comes upon you, and you will be My witnesses in *Jerusalem*, and in all *Judea* and *Samaria*, and *to the ends of the earth.*"(Acts 1:8 BSB) These are physical places that exist today. So therefore the seal of Victory and Ownership of the Eternal Father by the Holy Spirit, is for you to obtain. Take hold of and be empowered by The Lord in this present moment in time…today! Our Heavenly Father ABSOLUTELY LOVES forgiving sin and He is ready to forgive any and every sin we have committed. Why does He love forgiving so much, you ask? Because God loves His creation, which is you. Yet our sinful nature (from birth) that initiates sin separates us from connecting with a holy God. But He wants us to be made right with Him so that the Holy Father and His creation who are made righteous in His Son Jesus can walk and fellowship with Him forever through faith. And with this amazing love from God, He however, calls us to turn from that forgiven sin that has been conquering us towards death. The Lord desires obedience by the power of His unconditional love. Just sit with God and call that sin out to Him as it really is; the way He sees it without making excuses for your actions. He will forgive you, dust you off, take you by the hand and begin to lead you in the way of His Son Jesus Christ. It is written, "For I desire mercy, not sacrifice, and acknowledgment of God rather than burnt offerings" (Hosea 6:6 NIV) What this means is that there was a time where Israel (the nation) was so caught up in sin, they had the false notion that the Lord would receive and be pleased with their sacrifices and burnt offerings (good works and being a "good" person) while having hearts that were willfully submitted to evil deeds or their own personal will. It was their version of the modern-day Saint Aloysius of Repetitive Repenting Confession Booths (no pun intended...I promise). The Lord wants nothing more than for you to walk in this life victoriously over mental illness and behavior health issues and any other heavy self-condemned thought life, being freed from every guilt and condemnation. Romans 8:1 KJV says, "There is no longer any condemnation, (neither for yourself nor towards anyone else) for those who are in Christ Jesus." This is how we need to do it. So, you can stop covering your sins and past hurts and pains, "bad thoughts", worries, depressions with the false sedatives of Satan and cover them fully with the Blood of the Lamb, Jesus Christ. Moses murdered an Egyptian in a presumptuous attempt to rescue God's people. Not only was Moses in the devil's hands, God knew what Moses did. Yet this is the man that God redeemed and sent to face Pharaoh to demand Pharaoh to release the children of God from the land and hands of bondage in Egypt. The children of Israel prospered and walked out of the land of Satan's idols. And the devil couldn't do anything about it. Confess your sins to God while asking Him to place them in front of your thoughts no matter how many they are.

Leave no rug unturned and leave every door of your heart and mind unlocked for Christ to enter. If you have to put lamps and new light bulbs in these dark places, do it. There is no greater time than right now at this very moment than to snitch on the devil and break his chains on you. Tell God what Satan has been doing to wreak your life because the devil has been definitely standing before the throne of God accusing and snitching on you! (Job 1:9 NASB, Job 1:11 NASB, Job 2:5 MSG) Therefore, when Christ comes into your house, He's not coming to judge you, He's coming to judge Satan by stomping on his head for bringing hell and destruction to your life. Pray and ask God to help you turn away from them quickly, immediately and get out of Egypt, the land of bondage.

Moments of Meditation

Here in this passage presents the heart of God concerning His desire for you to be made whole, clean and be in right standing with Him through repentance from now and unto eternal life with Him. Think about, sit with these and meditate on these words until you know God and His heart for you. Dissect them until they fit securely into your heart. Pray and ask Him if necessary, to clarify what you need or want to know more about Him. Then thank and praise God for simply who He is...

> *"But do not forget this one thing, dear friends: With the Lord a day is like a thousand years, and a thousand years are like a day. The Lord is not slow in keeping his promise, as some understand slowness. Instead he is patient with you, not wanting anyone to perish, but everyone to come to repentance. 2 Peter 3:8-9 NLT*

God is not slack in showing observable signs of His return because He's not coming- but rather He has the patience of eternity and love that cannot be measured by human understanding.

And He is not slack in bringing you into complete authority over mental illness but in the midst of it, God will be nurturing you until you are assured of God's unwavering love and power over all things in this world through Christ Jesus. He desires to snatch and adopt as many children from the World and its mentality to become His very own before their freewill expires. Repentance is not separate from humility and is a precondition of God's grace and mercy. Before the sacrifice of Jesus Christ was complete, sacrifices of animals only covered presumptuous sins. But these kind are of the worst of sins that "forces" God's grace in presuming that The Lord will forgive even though you know a particular sin is wrong. Sins we willfully commit but did not know were sins. After the fall and before reconciliation, every intentional and premeditated sin and the guilt of it was to remain on your head and conscience to live with. Thank you, Lord! Through Jesus, He has lifted the guilt from our consciences and the eternal consequence of our sins, and that the condemnation has been overruled and overturned by our True Judge through the Attorney and Mediator for our souls!

Stepping Inside Jericho

There are several scripture references in this chapter that are a gift from the Lord for us to take hold of as we war against the attacks of the enemy or digest the conviction of the Holy Spirit. God's Spirit will let us know through conviction and studying our bibles that we need to repent and talk to him about specific actions that do not line up with His will. Hate the consequence of not repenting so much to the point where we ask God daily if there are any sins we've committed that we need to confess and declare that we will be obedient to His revelation. Keep a clean record with God through faith in His Son Jesus Christ and walk with God inside of His promise.

I Am The Sum of God's Love

Not the sum of my past...
Stop...
Now what I would like for you to do is I want you to read that statement again just to make sure you're not just reading it, but you've actually received it...Repeat the words again: "I am the sum of God's love...not the sum of my past."

Now for about 2-3 minutes (or longer if need be) remain quiet and just sit with this statement asking God to confirm what was just said. After you read this sentence, write down some brief personal thoughts that has warred and is continuously warring against your mind on a daily basis. And ask God to look them over. Off the top of my head, let's see if I can accurately I.D. the human nature of the people that God has used and called for a specific purpose throughout scripture...

Noah during serving God became in a drunken state - but he was seen a righteous man in God's eyes and was called to build the Ark to save his family from the flood. Abraham, Isaac and Jacob were all fearful liars in some way, shape or form (Jacob showed favoritism to Joseph above his brothers) - yet through these came God's Chosen People. Moses was a stuttering murderer (he stuck and killed an Egyptian with his bare hands) – or at least he couldn't speak very well- yet he was called by The Lord to face Pharaoh a bunch of times to tell him to release God's people from Egypt's captivity, to lead millions of complaining Israelites to the Red Sea and part it so they could walk through it to journey to the Promised

Land. But since the Children of Israel where not ready to be a nation and needed to be weaned off of the influences of the Egyptian culture God caused Moses to circle a mountain through the wilderness for 40 years... with millions of complaining Israelites who finally arrived at The Promised Land. (Moses could not enter the Promised Land because he was tired of... well, the millions of complaining Israelites asking for water so he struck the rock (which God did not command him to do so) and going over that will take the conversation to a different path...like Moses did opposed to the millions of complaining Israelites who were now happy Israelites after finally making it to the Promised Land.)

Rahab was a prostitute yet through her loins came the Messiah Jesus Christ.

Gideon was (in his mind) a fearful and powerless man, hiding in the basement beating out wheat in the wine press while the Midianites were destroying and taking everything from Israel- but the angel of the Lord called him a mighty warrior of valor and blessed Gideon to defeat the thousands of the Midianites, Amalekites and the sons of the East with only 300 men- by shouting from the top of a valley.

Samson served God as a powerful judge of Israel, mighty in human strength killing thousands of Philistines at different times, yet he was flawed to the point of his demise with a gullible heart to one name Delilah.

Samuel, a prophet and priest of God, had a knack for choosing kings based on how good they looked rather than them being fit to be a godly king. God had to intervene the second time around when choosing a king for Israel after Samuel's first choice failed miserably and eternally.

David not only took Bathsheba from Uriah, he impregnated her during the war that Uriah was fighting for the king. Then, in order to cover it up David had Uriah placed on the front line of the most heated area of the war so he could be killed-and he was which in God's eyes was murder.

...Yet, from the loins of David- the man known as Jesus Christ.

Peter - a 3-time denier of Christ Jesus yet he was given the keys to the Kingdom of God - the Church

Paul – a persecutor and destroyer (murderer) of Christians...yet God chose him to carry the Gospel of Christ to the Gentiles, writing some 13 letters or books of the New Testament which all focuses on the building up of and edification for children of God moving us to because mature men and women of God.

Mary – caught in the act of prostitution by Pharisees but forgiven directly by Christ.

The Man at the caves – under the condemnation and power of "Legion" being tormented day and night...yet Jesus Christ stepped from the shore to the tormented soul and commanded the legion of demons to leave the man and they had no choice but to leave and fled to the swine.

Afterwards, the man went into town he formally lived outside of and his new character amazed everyone because he was fully clothed and in his right mind through the redeeming power of Christ Jesus.

Now about your past...about what you are going through...

Just as these weren't thrown away, you too are salvageable and valued in the Lord's eyes. Your past does not determine who God is. God is in the soul-refurbishing business, the renewing-your-mind business, the tossing-your-sins-in-the-sea-of-forgetfulness business, the sending-His-word-into-your-life-and-healing-you business. Your. Sins. Have. Been. Forgiven. Through. Jesus. Christ. Period. Now walk in it. You. Are. Valued. And. Loved. By. The. Almighty. God. Receive it.

Anything you hear that doesn't sound like that or shies away from that truth- the truth is not in that person.

I AM the sum of God's love...and not the sum of my past

But Why?

Because you were made for Him. You are fearfully and wonderfully made, every hair on your head is numbered. You out of all creation are His prize possession and masterpiece and He proved that He was willing to do anything to redeem you from the pit, from Sheol, from lies of the enemy, from in the front of His seat of judgement, from eternal separation...BUT DO YOU RECEIVE THIS? Does this truth now belong to you? Take hold of this and make it yours as you walk towards and in the victory and promises through Christ Jesus.

...Equals 490

Wondering what the significance of the number 490 is and what numbers are multiplied together to equal this total amount? 70 multiplied by 7 equals 490. The word multiplied or rather "times" should be a beginning hint to where this chapter is going. The Bible reads,

Then Peter came and said to Him, "Lord, how often shall my brother sin against me and I forgive him? Up to seven times?" Jesus said to him, "I do not say to you, up to seven times, but up to seventy times seven. The main topic of focus in this chapter is forgiveness. Now some translations read as "70 times" others "70 times seven" and others say "77 times".

Whether the lesser number is the correct number amount to forgive or the other through multiplication, Christ calls us to forgive in all truth and to do it excessively, freely and as often as we can not only because God will forgive us if we do the same for others (Matthew 18:23,27 ESV, Matthew 18:21 NASB, Mark 11:26 AMPV) but Scripture says that, "For this reason the kingdom of heaven may be compared to a king who wished to settle accounts with his slaves- Matt 18:23 NASB. Then it says, "...And the lord of that slave felt compassion and released him and forgave him the debt – Matt 18:27 NASB. The kingdom of heaven possesses blessings in overwhelming abundance AND is fully and completely accessible to the believer who sets his heart towards pleasing The Lord, which in some instances means to decrease and suffer for the sake of gaining Christ. The Lord establishes kings on the earth and this king is who he is because God placed him there... but let's not lose track, even though that statement is truth. The results of settling accounts with slaves who became slaves through offensive actions in the context of God's desire are to have compassion...release them (from the incarceration cells of your heart) ...and forgive the debt. Sometimes, whether Christian or not, that's not an easy pill to swallow. In Biblical interpreted sense, anyone struggling to or who refuses to forgive (release) another person for the sins committed against them casts the violator into their own personal Sheol and holding cell within their own heart and mind, to rot until they pay the penalty. Yet the persecuted warden of the cell, when harboring offense after offense over long periods of time, out of ignorance only inflicts grave sickness upon himself or herself. Psychologically by human nature at times, those who trespass against us are sentenced to death by us, because the flesh through the curse of sin can only do what has been given authority to do – that is to self-destruct. Unfortunately, in this severe case, the mind and heart will almost always be led to both spiritual and mental illness due to the festering of the inward parts of the human being. Yet when we release our afflicters (or ask the Lord to help us release them and forgive their trespasses), the Holy Spirit does a clean sweep as often as we ask Him (emptying out our spiritual concentration camps and in fact allowing God to wash and do a thorough maintenance to our soul and spirit completely. This is an important component towards breaking the chains of mental illness/spiritual oppression. Step by step God places our lives back in order, instilling the perfect peace of God to our life, purity in heart with a clean conscience enabling us to live the abundant life offered through Jesus Christ.

Moments of Meditation

"Then said Jesus, Father, forgive them; for they know not what they do. And they parted his raiment and cast lots." Luke 23:34 KJV

The next time we have the opportunity to experience the sinful actions of mankind throughout the world, including those committed against you and those you've committed against others, we witness that the opposition to forgiveness is actually judgement and vengeance, not refusing to forgive. This too is a tactic and temptation of the enemy in that when we refuse to forgive, we then become judges, and when we judge we make a presumptuous move to exonerate God from His throne and take it for ourselves (as Satan desired to do - Isaiah 14:13-

14 KJV) and due to our sin nature, more than not we will have the tendency to judge in unrighteousness which will bear further consequences (Isaiah 14:17-21 NIV). Now when we take the time to meditate on these words of Christ on the cross, He truly meant that men do not know what they are doing, literally- because men by nature are spiritually blind and creatures of impulse. Mankind apart from Jesus Christ through the Holy Spirit are completely controlled by their own flesh, selfish impulses and sinful desires. Now of course that does not mean we turn a blind eye of acceptance to such sinful behaviors, but rather it provides a basic revelation of the reason why we are called to forgive. It's comparable to a 3-year-old with a horrible father who has set his thoughts to teach that child to do every evil under the sun until adulthood. That child who is then now in adulthood can only carry out the actions instilled in himself to do since youth because that's all he knows to do. Make no mistake due to the importance of living life apart from unnecessary conviction, internal conflict and condemnation, here, we will evaluate three scriptures containing the teachings of Jesus in regard to forgiveness. The main purpose is to acquire wisdom, understanding and to see mankind the way Christ sees us and our situation. These are the scriptures:

"For if you forgive others for their transgressions, your Heavenly Father will also forgive you. But if you do not forgive others, then your Father will not forgive your transgressions." Matthew 6:14-15 NASB

There is one enemy of our soul and that is Satan. Unfortunately, how Satan works is that he works through the uncovered and unarmored areas of our character and life and disguises himself behind the scenes while influencing the mind, heart and actions of man. (Please take the time to study Romans 7:13-25 NLT/NASB - these passages give an example of the war mankind face within themselves and the necessity of praying for and forgiving others).1 Peter 5:8 NLT says,

"Stay alert! Watch out for your great enemy, the devil. He prowls around like a roaring lion, looking for someone to devour. Stand firm against him and be strong in your faith.

Remember that your Christian brothers and sisters all over the world are going through the same kind of suffering you are."

Based on this passage, if disregarded, are several areas of opportunity where the devil chooses to attack and devour. The first is lacking discernment and wisdom thus not being alert and sober in spirit. Wisdom and discernment is seeing everything in life from God's point of view which can only be acquired by asking Him for this. (1 Kings 3:9, 10 ESV) and (Matthew 7:11 NASB)

The next point to understand is that the devil loves to prowl around your life or to move in sneaky manner while hunting you for the kill, with camouflage being one of his top choice weapons. But Ephesians 4:27 ESV says, "and give no opportunity to the devil." Absolutely no area of your life - especially in unforgiving.

Another is the lack of power in our life through spiritual malnutrition. Revitalize and overflood (yes, I made that up) yourself with God's presence by taking the time to sit, talk with and listen to God in prayer. Study and meditate on His word often throughout the day. Let me rephrase that statement, start your morning off with spending time with God first thing in the morning and don't step out of the house without asking Him to lead you throughout the day. Praise and thank Him daily for the victories that He has planned for you in the future.

"But love your enemies, and do good, and lend, expecting nothing in return; and your reward will be great, and you will be sons of the Most High; for He Himself is kind to ungrateful and evil men. Be merciful, just as your Father is merciful. "Do not judge, and you will not be judged; and do not condemn, and you will not be condemned; pardon, and you will be pardoned. Luke 6:35-37 NASB

Mercy in the Mirror

Forgive yourself.

Please forgive yourself.

The person you see when you look in the mirror knows that they didn't do everything right. They weren't always truthful. They weren't always faithful or caring in their words or actions and have said and done some horrible things they aren't able to retract. Maybe they didn't show the love or give the time that they should have to their spouse, mom or dad, siblings or children and this decision proved to be costly. Maybe it's because they weren't shown the right way to love. They've made some horrible mistakes in their life that they now cannot seem to get over. The truth is that we can't get over our past sins, failures and mistakes. We have to hand them over. For 2 Corinthians 7:10 NIV says that, "Godly sorrow brings repentance that leads to salvation and leaves no regret, but worldly sorrow brings death." Self-condemnation brings self-condemnation. And a person is never condemned to life, but rather to death. I remember I arrived at a point in my life to where the weight of the guilt of my sins were too heavy to carry. Not only that, but I began isolating myself and hiding but I couldn't run from God any longer. I found myself not being able to look at the man in the mirror without breaking apart.

Yet 2 Corinthians 5:21 NLT says, For God made Christ, who never sinned, to be the offering for our sin, so that we could be made right with God through Christ.

Jesus took our place, he took our guilt and shame and placed it on himself and offered us His righteousness so that we longer have to carry condemnation in our hearts. Believe you me, that forgiving yourself is an important part of being sanctified, and sanctification is long process- possibly even lifelong. Romans 8:1 NKJV says, *"There is* therefore now no condemnation to those who are in Christ Jesus, who do not walk according to the flesh, but according to the Spirit." So, if God in the flesh is willing to forgive you completely, wiping away all sin and holding no condemnation towards you, who are we to stand in God's way by condemning ourselves? Forgiving yourself isn't always easy - but it's always necessary to become who God is calling you to be.

Forgive.

Bad Company Corrupts God Character

Three important factors in your healing and victory from mental depravity, illness and depression is removing yourself and from your atmosphere, diameter and home, toxic and negative people or their influence thereof. Love the person. Abhor their ways. The second can be worse than the first if we refuse to clean house on this one, which is to rid and wash your mind from the negative thoughts, presumptions and imaginations that the enemy is "accompanying" you with. The third may sound like a broken record but these choice morsels are vital to your continued healing: fill the empty spaces in your mind and life once cleaning begins with Christ Jesus, His Spirit (the Holy Spirit) AND with believers and people who will speak into with the wisdom of God in their heart. Before writing this chapter, The Spirit led me to and reminded me of a number of instances in the Scriptures that I've studied over time to pull from that supports and relates to the topic of this chapter to help me build it up for our desired wisdom, knowledge and exhortation. So, let's get started.

First, mental illness and depravity for the most part in its foundational initiation in our lives and within my experience with God guiding me towards overcoming it, is spiritual. It's initial sowing or implantation may have come from a physical violation towards you or negative experience that has festered within. You could be holding on to something (possibly destructive) or someone (not right for you) or some belief system (that may be carnal and self-limiting in nature) that God is calling you to let go of. Yes, it is also scriptural to where this particular illness or "possession "has come into being from the results of having made a conscientious decision to store up sin and disobedience in the flesh to the breaking point of "fullness"; but none the less mental illness is spiritual. Yet, to stay on course let's visit some scripture references to where our relationships with friendships, family members and our personal habits can promote the "pulling away" from the creation and character that God desires for us to have.

"Now King Solomon loved many foreign women along with the daughter of Pharaoh: Moabite, Ammonite, Edomite, Sidonian, and Hittite women, from the nations concerning which the LORD had said to the sons of Israel, "You shall not associate with them, nor shall they associate with you, for they will surely turn your heart away after their gods." Solomon held fast to these in love." 1 Kings 11:1-2 NASB

Now though this story concerning King Solomon in its context talks about the influences of foreign women, the spiritual revelation and underlining surface of the passage is that there is an ideology or ideologies that exist and dwell within the hearts of people who do not know the Lord (nor care to know Him) on this earth that is in fact "foreign" and is in opposition to the truth of the Gospel, The Word of God. Their ideology is worldly and godless at its core and these beliefs can have a negative impact on our relationship with our Heavenly Father and His perfect plans for our lives, even to the point of self- destruction. Let's continue further in scripture concerning the character of King Solomon:

"For Solomon went after Ashtoreth the goddess of the Sidonians and after Milcom the detestable idol of the Ammonites. Solomon did what was evil in the sight of the LORD, and did not follow the LORD fully, as David his father had done. Then Solomon built a high place for Chemosh the detestable idol of Moab, on the mountain which is east of Jerusalem, and for Molech the detestable idol of the sons of Ammon. Thus, also he did for all his foreign wives, who burned incense and sacrificed to their gods. 1 Kings 11:5-8 NASB

So here is godly knowledge and discernment: Satan hides himself within the worldly popularities of a particular time period until it becomes outdated in the eyes of that time period's society. Then he goes "to and fro on the earth" and "back and forth on it", to see where and how else he might wreak more havoc on the unaware. So, what then is the modern-day representation of the gods that King Solomon then bowed himself to? Ashtoreth is to modern-day pornography, sexually immorality and fornication as Milcom and Molech is to modern forms of child abortion and trafficking as Chemosh is to human sacrifice such as violence related to organized crime syndicates, gangs and nocturnal societies. And Solomon agreed to allow these to remain in the presence of God. So now Solomon, being made the wisest king to ever live by The Lord God Himself (because Christ had not yet come), even his wisdom alone was not enough to shield him from the spiritual draining of intertwining himself with and to the wrong kinds of hearts and minds. This is truth in saying: you can have all the godly wisdom in the world, but it does not mean anything unless the fear of the Lord (highest reverence and regards over everyone and everything else) comes first (Proverbs 9:10 NASB) and no amount of learning can protect you when you refuse to obey God. And the instruction, thus wisdom of God was for Solomon to remove from himself, the foreign women, the association of foreign thinking and beliefs or else his heart would be turned away. He did not listen to the one who made Him wise among men. So, consequences did follow. This is one of my favorite scriptures: Psalm 1:1-6 NIV that says:

Blessed is the one who does not walk in step with the wicked or stand in the way that sinners take or sit in the company of mockers but whose delight is in the law of the Lord, and who meditates on his law day and night. That person is like a tree planted by streams of water, which yields its fruit in season and whose leaf does not wither— whatever they do prospers. Not so the wicked! They are like chaff that the wind blows away Therefore the wicked will not stand in the judgment, nor sinners in the assembly of the righteous. For the Lord watches over the way of the righteous, but the way of the wicked leads to destruction.

We have to be careful when choosing our company in which we associate with: for one group of people can lead and direct us towards life and another set of company can lead us to death. Choose wisely. Choose Life.

The next issues are the thoughts and accusations the enemy attempts to accompany us with in order to bring about confusion and mental restlessness.

You imagine being in the presence of God as you open the Bible and you ask, "God, what are your thoughts concerning me personally?" ...He looks back as a loving Father and He asks, "How much time do you have?" He then speaks and points you to specific scriptures that explains His heart towards you and how to respond through the love and knowledge of God:

> *"Before I formed you in the womb I knew you; Before you were born I sanctified[a] you; I [b]ordained you a prophet to the nations." Jeremiah 1:5 NKJV*

> *"I will praise You, for I am fearfully and wonderfully made, Marvelous are Your works, and that my soul knows very well." Psalm 139:14 NKJV* (unfortunately many souls do not know)

> *"What is mankind that you are mindful of them, human beings that you care for them? You have made them a little lower than the angels and crowned them with glory and honor. You made them rulers over the works of your hands; you put everything under their feet: all flocks and herds, and the animals of the wild, the birds in the sky, and the fish in the sea, all that swim the paths of the seas." Psalm 8:4-8 NIV*

> *"So be strong and courageous! Do not be afraid and do not panic before them. For the LORD your God will personally go ahead of you. He will neither fail you nor abandon you." Deuteronomy 31:6 NLT*

> *"Truly I tell you," Jesus replied, "no one who has left home or brothers or sisters or mother or father or children or fields for me and the gospel will fail to receive a hundred times as much in this present age: homes, brothers, sisters, mothers, children and fields—along with persecutions—and in the age to come eternal life." Mark 10: 29-30 NIV*

> *For I know the plans I have for you," declares the LORD, "plans to prosper you and not to harm you, plans to give*

*you hope and a future. The LORD your God is with you,
the Mighty Warrior who saves. He will take great delight
in you; in his love he will no longer rebuke you but will
rejoice over you with singing." Zephaniah 3:17 NIV*

"But God, being rich in mercy, because of the great love with which he loved us, even when we were dead in our trespasses, made us alive together with Christ— by grace you have been saved." Ephesians 2:4-5 ESV

On and on and on...

We can both be here ministering to the Lord and cutting the enemy and his accusations in half and to pieces all day long if you like. How much time you got? Jot these down in your personal journal and make sure your soul knows these very well. - Jeremiah 29:11 NASB/NKJV

The Bible is full of precious treasuries and at the same time is similar to a state-of-the-art medical facility and wellness center. But when dealing with the deep issues of life that are having its way with us in our minds and hearts, the correct surgery and medicine needs to be administered accurately, immediately and consistently until the wounds are treated and the area of your spiritual body is fortified through the knowledge of Christ and what He has done for us on Calvary. He died for us to break every chain, open every eye and to free every captive of Satan. Let me repeat this so you hear me clearly. Every chain broken. Every eye opened. Every captive set free. Now what did we just do in the previous scriptures as we walked through a mock trial and responded to an accusation of the devil? The scripture reads: "For though we walk in the flesh, we do not war according to the flesh, for the weapons of our warfare are not of the flesh, but divinely powerful for the destruction of fortresses. We are destroying speculations and every lofty thing raised up against the knowledge of God, and we are taking every thought captive to the obedience of Christ."

2 Corinthians 10:3-5 NASB

In other words, though we are living in the physical realm called Earth, as God's children we are to recognize that we are citizens of Heaven (and those who have yet but will now soon believe in Christ Jesus as well) and

God our King dwells in us and wherever the King goes so does His Kingdom accompany Him and since He is in us through Christ, so does the Kingdom accompany us. Therefore, the Holy arsenals of the heavenly barracks are freely and abundantly supplied to us to wreak havoc and destruction on the works of hell in our lives and on those works of the devil in this life. Yet be confident that our Helper, His ammunition and armor along with the Armies of God is in infinite supply. Infinite supply. All are standing by waiting for your orders...

Filling the gaps

Once the cleaning begins on your mind, heart, and physical diameter or circle, in order to continue to prosper in our healing, we have to immediately fill those gaps and empty spaces with the things of God, the thoughts of God and the people of God. Previously we have went over the words of God's heart towards and how it should be when counter attacking hellish accusations of the enemy and replacing those lies with the love and truth of God and Christ Jesus. As we strive forward in this manner, we will avoid the consequences of not filling the gaps explained by Jesus in the following passage of scripture: The Lord says,

"When an evil spirit leaves a person, it goes into the desert, seeking rest but finding none. Then it says, 'I will return to the person I came from.' So, it returns and finds its former home empty, swept, and in order. Then the spirit finds seven other spirits more evil than itself, and they all enter the person and live there. And so that person is worse off than before. That will be the experience of this evil generation." Matthew 12:43-45 NLT

Ever heard of relapse? And then someone dying from relapse because they went back into the same bondage they were delivered from? Because there was nothing in place to replace the empty space that was strong enough to resist the temptation to return to the bondage that was there before. So, when the enemy is received back into your atmosphere, to keep you from "escaping" again, he moves in forcefully and swiftly as a prowling predator to take your life before having the chance of being rescued.

Or,

Have you ever been on the receiving end of a spiritual violation and you have come to terms that the violation was not your fault? And when you did not feel that empty space with truth and expectation you found yourself going from blaming yourself to not trusting anyone on outside of yourself to blaming every other person that you've come in contact with in your life who could've done something about it, who reminds you of the person or people who hurt you? This person has been left off as the scripture says worse than before because you go from the extreme of self-hating to the other extreme of simply hating distrusting and anger then leading to hurting others who had nothing to with the pain that you feel. Be watchful of the enemy's tactics for the devil is trying to isolate you through your emotions to take your life while reducing the possibility of the rescued.

"The Hymostphere" Part I

I may not have shared this, but I'm a fairly creative person. In 2005, I was attending a community college in Downtown Cleveland, Ohio majoring in Recording Arts Technology. I always had music in my mind as a young boy and would be often heckled by childhood friends for imitating the sounds of music in my head...out loud. I guess it sounded like annoying noises to them. My mother tried to get me to play drums and the saxophone - but these instruments didn't sound like what I was used to hearing on my hip hop cassette tapes. Yet attending this music program was the catalyst for getting everything musical out of me. I also learned that you don't need a million-dollar studio to start creating music, which I found out from one of my friends who was also in the music program. He told me what I needed to purchase to make music the "new way". So, I took his advice because I didn't have $1500 laying around the house to purchase a piece of equipment, as a professor suggested, that would prove to be useless by next year. I went to a music store in a suburb of Cleveland and purchased some equipment on credit (in which I paid back immediately as soon as I received the funds from my school grants). On the Eastside of Cleveland in my mom's attic, I set up the electronic music equipment I purchased from the music store, I downloaded a digital music software program that another friend who created hip hop music let me borrow on my computer- sharing is caring- and I started making hip hop instrumental music or as we call them, beats. I used to make those hard, sinister and dark instrumental tracks. I really can't listen to them now because I'm no longer in that space of emotions or atmosphere anymore- plus they are horrible creative-wise. In creativity, it's difficult to replicate anything other than what's inside your heart. Eventually, in 2006, I moved out to Southern California to possibly do something with music production. It's a competitive environment in LA so I started producing more instrumental tracks to build a catalog to get noticed in the music world to no avail while I worked my day job. Eventually, January 2009, I landed a music marketing internship with a major record company and I ended up discovering a ton of new music that was different from the music I was used to listening to in Cleveland. I met other creative-minded people, I loved the vibe there, and I even enjoyed hopping from train to train to get from Orange County to LA. As a young producer, there was a lot of music to digest and listen and some of these styles of music I began to incorporate into my own music creativity. I stayed there for about nine months until finally my internship was ended. I would call myself making connections with people to stay inside of the company but after a while, though I enjoyed interning there more so than my paid job- it still kind of seemed like a dead end as well. But anyways, moving fast forward, by 2012, I had been moving out of the mental illness atmosphere and I had truly dedicated my life to Christ Jesus – now I still had some growing to do but still. What happened is that since my heart and mind was under God's reconstruction, my creative style and taste in electronic music, what "I" wanted to hear and how "I" wanted it to sound, had changed as well. So, as I was continuously creating, I ended up independently releasing an electronic instrumental album called "Midnight Automatik" under my moniker, "Kapatarus" in 2013.Well, one of the guys I went to school with in my last semester at Long Beach City College, who also mixed the album, invited me to do alive internet radio show/interview in LA. The interview was chill, and I got the chance to see how it feels to be the artist who talks a little bit about his creative process unrehearsed. At the radio show was another group of artists who interviewed after me while I sat in a chair off camera to just kind of observe and hang out. But after the interview session, I'll never forget what one of the other artists said to me who listened to my album before meeting me. He was like, "Your album was dope man, it's like...it's almost like you were coming from a spiritual place. Is that where you were coming from or thinking when you created the album??"

Then I, kind of pondering briefly on his comment, and though still not completely sure I understood why my music spoke to him in that way being that it was solely an instrumental album, said, "Yea, man, I was just creating what came out. Thank you, I'm glad you liked it." Years later, while sharing my testimony with different people I'd come in contact with, spending time with God in His Word and spending TONS of sabbatical time in different places around the OC (Orange County), I would find myself using this phrase a lot: the atmosphere. It was the only word I could think of in order to describe the way I viewed my perception of my surroundings in the season of mental illness and now the perception of my surroundings in my life being completely focused on God in Christ Jesus.

...Then the Holy Spirit reminded me of the portion of the Lord's Prayer, *Matthew 6:10 NASB*

> *"Your kingdom come. Your will be done,*
> *on earth as it is in heaven."*

And also, the King James Version interchanges the word "On" for "In". "Thy kingdom come. Thy will be done in earth, as it is in heaven."

And since we not only live on the planet Earth, but were also formed from the dust of the earth,

Therefore, the Kingdom of Heaven and the seeds and fruit of it can dwell not only around us... by the Holy Spirit through Christ Jesus *It can dwell upon us… And not only "on" us… The atmosphere of heaven will dwell "in" us…* There are phrases I like to remind myself of that goes like:

"God's presents are only found in His presence."

And this analogy:

"A king is always accompanied by his kingdom's representatives."

The "spiritual place" that the other artist spoke of when he heard my music was the connection and friendship between I and the Spirit of God and the desires dwelling in Heaven, the Kingdom of God, while on Earth, living and active inside me.

The longer we are in the atmosphere of the life promised by Christ Jesus and the longer we stay in God's presence, any other atmosphere that is outside or in opposition to the presence and power of God must go; it must surrender.

Mental illness and behavior health issues and the causes of these, has to surrender in the presence of God.

For it is written, *"He who is in you (being Christ Jesus) is greater than he who is in the world."* John 4:4 ESV

Discern that the remedies, troubles or pleasures of the world can in no way compare to or compete with the riches in Christ Jesus in the *heavenly places…*

"The Hymostphere" Part II

Hymostphere (h'eye/ most/fear) –

Spiritual/Wordplay: A particular type of atmosphere or space, both personal and isolated from distractions, dedicated to the one-on-one meeting and fellowship with the presence of God for instruction, worship, prayer, study and meditation.

Explaining "The Hymostphere"

During my rejuvenation from mental illness, I had several places where God and I would hangout and meet. There were green parks and beaches I would visit frequently. I had several break locations at my places of employment. I established *our* time at certain art museums. I sought and still seek Him while up in the early hours of the morning when it's still dark and it seems like everyone in the city is still sleeping. I draw near to God while painting biblical scriptures on my balcony. I pursue the *sound* and *feel* of His presence in my heart while creating music and a several other places if that wasn't enough already. It's not meant to come across as some sort of holier-than-thou boast. And it's also not so much as just simply having different "hangout" places with God. I just *needed* to have my alone time with Him and to be honest, I still do. A taste of this peace; His peace and reconciliation took hold of my soul. It *did not* exist in anything, any place or anyone else, only in the son Jesus. And this was and still *is* "The Business". When I found *this* treasure hidden in the field, I *bought* the field. It then became, in my heart, a necessity, to be crushed, transformed and renewed often without distractions in Christ, to see, know and take hold of the specific characteristics and promises of my Heavenly Father, His presence and His working hand in nature. All the while, I moved to perceive more clearly *His* atmosphere, past the natural atmosphere around me, to reside continuously on holy ground. And I sought and still do seek fellowship while witnessing His Word in life as being *truth* and *alive*. I know that was a bit much, so an example will always help. Take the beach for example that I love to visit and Sabbath at, especially in the winter months because (spoiler alert) no one ever goes to the beach in the winter, so you can hear everything in nature, including God speak in that still soft voice. When I'm there, I'm witnessing everything that God said was not made by things that were seen but unseen. Everything I see that is in regards to nature was created by the hands of God using *spiritual* material. The sand is the same material that God told Abraham his descendants will compare with numerically, as well as the stars in the sky. The beach waters are those that proceeded from the mouth of God in which also have been commanded to not surpass its boundaries of authority. The sun and the sunlight I see was designed by the hand of God to give physical light and has been commanded to rise and set in the proper direction at the proper time of day and season. The seagulls I see diving in and out of the water for the food of their choice at the beach are in likeness to the birds that Jesus taught us to examine when life tempts us to worry. Hopefully, you understand where I'm coming from. The point I'm making is this: as we began to draw as close as we can to God, everything we now experience in life seemingly points back to God and His word. I love these places because I could literally get lost in the Word of God, interpreting scripture, meditation, sometimes for hours, seeing the visions from God and fragments of His plans for my life. There is a particular kind of peace of God in these places that the soul desires more of and they cannot be purchased yet the places are intentionally chosen and freely available, (And no, I cannot share mines with you. You have to find your own. Just kidding… kind of). I even found myself preaching, teaching and ministering out loud in my space because the Spirit of God was overflowing in me, so everything had to come out. And the outpour filled the atmosphere. There was the late Dr. Myles

Monroe who said, "The reason why they can't find the Garden of Eden is because Eden wasn't a place, it was an atmosphere." The presence of God. And when Adam sinned in the Garden, and sin entered the world, God then placed Cherubim and a flaming sword to guard against the way to the Tree of Life. In other words, God removed man from His presence or atmosphere because sin and He Who is Holy cannot coexist together. The atmosphere of God is now abundantly available through the Man and Tree of Life, Christ Jesus, by the power of the Flaming Sword that once guarded the Tree of Life, The Holy Spirit. We have access to the atmosphere of God whenever we like, just set your heart to meet and find God's presence and He'll meet you face to face. I cannot stress how important it was for me to have a place or places like these when struggling with mental illness. But once you know how and where to meet with God, you will never want to forget.

Moments of Meditation

I remember lying on the sands of the beach one day just letting time pass by resting in the Lord for the remainder of the day, watching the sun go down and the ocean waters sway back-and-forth, from a distance you could see the hills on Catalina Island. There were some people enjoying themselves with their family and friends and it was the conclusion of a smooth day. Then a little bit to my left and I saw maybe about 5 to 7 seagulls resting in the sand themselves: They were watching the waters of the ocean crash on shore and go back-and-forth, watching the sun go down, I noticed that when the air hit their face, they'd squints their eyes and their feathers would blow about their bodies and they were just relaxing. And then it made me wonder: Do they even have a care in the world? I wondered if they had the same fears and anxieties that we humans have. Of course, it would be ignorant of me to become jealous and envious of their resolve, being that we are created in the image of God, but they seemed to be creatures who have achieved in this moment still peace that mankind has yet to understand or have knowledge of. They seem to have an understanding of the knowledge of God and the peace of his atmosphere more so than I had ever experience. But they encouraged me and reminded me: keep your trust and your faith steadfast towards the presence of the Heavenly Father who loves you. I could only ask God to give me a kind of faith and trust in Him that allows me to rest in His perfect peace all the days of my life. I was then reminded of the passage Jesus taught in Matthew 6:25-34 NIV "Therefore I tell you, do not worry about your life, what you will eat or drink; or about your body, what you will wear. Is not life more than food, and the body more than clothes? Look at the birds of the air; they do not sow or reap or store away in barns, and yet your heavenly Father feeds them. Are you not much more valuable than they? Can any one of you by worrying add a single hour to your life? "And why do you worry about clothes? See how the flowers of the field grow. They do not labor or spin. Yet I tell you that not even Solomon in all his splendor was dressed like one of these. If that is how God clothes the grass of the field, which is here today and tomorrow is thrown into the fire, will he not much more clothe you—you of little faith? So, do not worry, saying, 'What shall we eat?' or 'What shall we drink?' or 'What shall we wear?' For the pagans run after all these things, and your heavenly Father knows that you need them. But seek first his kingdom and his righteousness, and all these things will be given to you as well. Therefore, do not worry about tomorrow, for tomorrow will worry about itself. Each day has enough trouble of its own.

Yea...God is the truth. Seek Him.

The Hymostphere Part III

"Heavenly Places"

One morning I was meditating on the scriptures and the things of God and I began thinking about all the ways Satan is trying to imitate God in this life and I made this little chart:

Imitation	Authentic
<u>Satan (Not God's equal/ desires the worship that belongs to God)</u>	<u>The Lord God</u>
666 (Seal or Mark of the Beast)	Seal of the Holy Spirit
False Prophet (Different Jesus)	Jesus Christ the Son of God
Main focus is Treasures of the World	Main focus is Treasures in Heaven
Worldly perspective and wisdom on life	God's perspective and wisdom
Faith in self or the flesh	Faith in Christ Jesus

Experience a "high" atmosphere using drugs, alcohol, sexual immorality, love of money, possessions, success	????????
Temporary	Permanent
Death	Alive/Life

One day I was praying for Holy Spirit's direction for a bible study and for the men that God would send to the group. And as I asked God what books we should read and study through together as one body in Christ the Lord said, "Ephesians." So, I said, "Ok, cool". As I started slowly reading and examining the first chapter of Ephesians, I sectioned around with red ink the first passage that caught my attention:

Ephesians 1:3-7 NASB

"Blessed be the God and Father of our Lord Jesus Christ, who has blessed us with every spiritual blessing in the *heavenly* places in Christ, just as He chose us in Him before the foundation of the world, that we would be holy and blameless before Him. In love He predestined us to adoption as sons through Jesus Christ to Himself, according to the kind intention of His will, to the praise of the glory of His grace, which He freely bestowed on us in the Beloved. In Him we have redemption through His blood, the forgiveness of our trespasses, according to the riches of His grace"

And Ephesians 1:18-21 NASB

"I pray that the eyes of your heart may be enlightened, so that you will know what is the hope of His calling, what are the riches of the glory of His inheritance in the saints, and what is the surpassing greatness of His power toward us who believe. These are in accordance with the working of the strength of His might which He brought about in Christ, when He raised Him from the dead and seated Him at His right hand in the *heavenly* places, far above all rule and authority and power and dominion, and every name that is named, not only in this age but also in the one to come."

And Then again in Ephesians 2:4-10 NASB

"But God, being rich in mercy, because of His great love with which He loved us, even when we were dead in our transgressions, made us alive together with Christ (by grace you have been saved), and raised us up with Him, and seated us with Him in the *heavenly* places in Christ Jesus, so that in the ages to come He might show the surpassing riches of His grace in kindness toward us in Christ Jesus. For by grace you have been saved through faith; and that not of yourselves, it is the gift of God; not as a result of works, so that no one may boast. For we are His workmanship, created in Christ Jesus for good works, which God prepared beforehand so that we would walk in them."

And Again Ephesians 3:10-11 NASB

"and to bring to light what is the administration of the mystery which for ages has been hidden in God who created all things; so that the manifold wisdom of God might now be made known through the church to the rulers and the authorities in the *heavenly* places. This was in accordance with the eternal purpose which He carried out in Christ Jesus our Lord, in whom we have boldness and confident access through faith in Him."

Heavenly places???

Whenever God mentions one thing in the Bible it's important enough already. If twice, then listen very closely. But three or more times? Highly crucial. Pay close attention because Christ doesn't want us to overlook this. We are living in a society where people desire to be placed on a pedestal, to be "stars", "praised and loved" by fans and other people. Where many would love to be overwhelmed by constant gratifications, rewards and the spotlight. Our flesh wants what it wants...but it wants whatever it wants *right now*. Our society needs to get to where it is going, and everything "needs" to be fast paced. If you slow things down or if *you* slow down, you're in the way. The unforeseen temptation though is to "Hurry up and die" or "Move quickly, before you miss what's least important in life." When it comes to inner turmoil and stress, we reach for the remedy that apparently produces the quickest results. Giving yourself more things to do so you don't have to think about issues in our world will not solve anything. I've experienced that feeling. I know people who still take that approach. In behavioral health issues many have resorted to using drugs and alcohol to pacify the emotions and stresses associated with deeper spiritual issues at hand. It is said that with drug usage such as heroine and crack cocaine, one can "achieve" a euphoric "high" for a little while and then crash, longing to feel that "atmosphere" once more. The addiction (and at times overdose) comes when the user attempts to "chase down" the first euphoric high first experienced but little do they know, or could care, will never realize that high again.

With the issues of alcohol, the desire to "escape" to a state of mind where the person doesn't feel the pain of internal and spiritual issues, but places them in a "floating" atmosphere, where one is thinking more of the temporal and imitational high, causes them to turn drinking into a habitual practice. Yet, these, the flesh, lead us to an atmosphere of death. But life in Christ Jesus lead us to and makes us aware of and alive with Him in the *heavenly places*. In order for us to fix the issues that appear to be on the surface of our physical realm, we must address and be able to navigate the "under the surface" atmosphere of our lives where our issues derive, known as the spiritual realm but in Christ Jesus. It is your own free will or choice whether or not you choose to believe my next statement but the truth in love is this: In the "under the surface" or unseen realm, *the heavenly places*, heaven and hell is continually at spiritual war- *and you are the grand prize*: the so-loved child to one side and the "trophy" to the other. In the laws of physics, every action has an equal and opposite reaction. And remember, since mental illness is *spiritual oppression* or *opposition*, it is also, while piggybacking off of the laws of physics, *a reaction from a spiritual action that was initiated in some way of some sort*. So yes, some of us may struggle with severe depression, addictions, or anxieties, but these are the *equal and opposite* or *opposing* reactions or better yet, results from actions committed or thoughts downloaded on or into our souls. The latter part of that statement is the broad answer as to why you are experiencing "this." Now bear with me and what I'm am about to disclose to you: in the spiritual realm, when you experience an attack or opposition, there are two ways that Satan, the enemy of our souls, would like for you to respond to his opposition or affliction. One, you will be tempted (never by the Lord God) to inflict the same or *equal* amount of pain *you are feeling and handling* on to the next person *or* further the affliction onto yourself. In this instance, Satan wants us to both cosign with and transfer that *opposing* and oppressive spirit (or the residue of it) on to the next person, with the expectation that next person spread it to the next person, and the next, so on and so forth. I'll call it the *spiritual conductivity through sin*. Two, with any afflicting action sent towards you by Satan, the intended purpose is to tempt you, the same way Job was tempted, to respond with an *opposing reaction* to God's supreme authority and His commands. But God's intended purpose for allowing Satan's affliction, and worldly hardship in our lives is for us to humble ourselves and surrender our hearts towards Him in Christ Jesus, so He can help us in our time of battle and to win our personal fight in the *heavenly places*. For Satan cannot beat or outbox God. For God the Son proved it on the cross at Calvary. Jesus Christ is the only one who has *the* victory and only in Him, will we fight armed *with* victory.

Moments of Meditation

Please excuse my lingo, religious community, but God is calling us to "get high" on this passage of scripture. I pray we come to a great understanding of this passage because when we do, we will be highly blessed and exhorted:

Grace and peace be multiplied to you in the knowledge of God and of Jesus our Lord; seeing that His divine power has granted to us everything pertaining to life and godliness, through the true knowledge of Him who called us by His own glory and excellence. For by these He has granted to us His precious and magnificent promises, so that by them you may become partakers of the divine nature, having escaped the corruption that is in the world by lust. 2 Peter 1: 2-4 NASB

The "Hymostphere" Concluded

When facing emotional pain or distress it's easy to isolate yourself. I know that's what I did when going through things, but it wasn't the best or wisest decision. It was a blessing I made it out despite the fact. But when going through difficult times, humble yourself and release the weight to Christ. Don't listen to the lies of Satan telling you not to "expose" yourself or "they don't care, nobody cares" or "I can do it on my own", "they are going to think you're weak", or "they are going to take advantage of you". Reject this false wisdom. We want to guard our hearts in life and at times it makes sense to not share everything with everyone, but we want to do this in the wisdom of God. God will tell us who, where and when. When Jesus' cousin, John the Baptist, was beheaded and killed for speaking the truth against King Herod's decision to marry his brother's wife it is written that, "When Jesus heard what had happened, he withdrew by boat privately to a solitary place. Hearing of this, the crowds followed him on foot from the towns." (Matthew 14:13 NIV)

Jesus was fully God as well as fully man and He felt heavy emotions just like we do today. So, Christ models to us that it's okay to find our place where we escape to fellowship with God but it's also equally important to know that we can do this also in the company of others because sometimes God will perform a miracle in the atmosphere where two or more are gathered. I remember in late February/early March I went on a retreat with a number of men of God from my church. I rode to Forest Falls, CA with two other brothers in Christ to the mountains which I, being city guy, had never been to the mountains nor did I have any intentions on going. Yet I must confess: it was the quietest and most serene place I had ever been in my entire life. You could hear absolutely everything in nature that would otherwise be muffled by the sounds of the city. It was here in the quietness and calm of the atmosphere where I could hear the still small voice of God more clearly. Being new husband, I received my instructions and exhortations from God concerning how to go about my marriage this first year, instructions on fatherhood and my growth in Him. So, I now understand the importance of "getting away" from the noise for a time to zero in on the fellowship with God in Christ Jesus.

I was conversing with a more seasoned Christian, husband and professional one day and he shared how he wakes up early in the morning, at like 4 A.M. to read God's Word, prays, then listens to worship music. After all these he then starts his day. When someone shares with me how they grow and start their day by being empowered with God's grace and peace, God is speaking to me on ways I can and need to grow. These are things I need to apply to my spiritual life to keep the fire of the Holy Spirit lit. I did try it and it felt like the whole world was sleeping and it was just me and God. I could hear His voice and instructions more clearly. I exhort: Find occasional solitude and your "Hymostphere" in the midst of your hurting or desires to know God more and to listen to the heart of God on every matter of your life. Sometimes, God will send someone or people your way for you to witness His blessing over you in the midst of your hurting or growing season. Fellowship with Him. Don't reject Him. He's for you. Not against you.

Lord, What Did I Do Wrong? Part I

Pure Gold.

Proverbs 27:21 ESV

"The crucible is for silver, and the furnace is for gold, and a man is tested by his praise."

And again,

Proverbs 17:3 AMP

"The refining pot is for silver and the furnace for gold, But the LORD tests hearts."

"I just "needed" to see if you call Me "good" because you're doing good...or if I'm good because I'm God."

- God

Lord, What Did I Do Wrong? Part II

The Lord Gives and Takes Away

1 John 4:4 NKJV

"You are of God, little children, and have overcome them, because
He who is in you is greater than he who is in the world."

"You didn't do anything wrong per se, I just needed
to shut Satan's mouth and remind him of who
I AM in you, and who you are in Me."

-God

Lord, What Did I Do Wrong? Part III

I'm your Heavenly Father,

Not a genie. And My love for you calls Me to correct and rebuke you as any father should do for the child he loves and finds pleasure in. Because if I don't correct you, then that's not true love and I'm agreeing with your self-destruction. And that is not what I desire.

-God

Lord, What Did I Do Wrong? Part IV

Even In The Fire

....Nebuchadnezzar, we have no need to defend our actions in this matter. We are ready for the test. If you throw us into the blazing furnace, then the God we serve is able to rescue us from a furnace of blazing fire and release us from your power, Your Majesty. But even if He does not, O king, you can be sure that we still will not serve your gods and we will not worship the golden statue you erected. Then Nebuchadnezzar was filled with wrath, and his facial expression was altered toward Shadrach, Meshach and Abed-nego. He answered by giving orders to heat the furnace seven times more than it was usually heated. He commanded certain valiant warriors who were in his army to tie up Shadrach, Meshach and Abed-nego in order to throw them into the furnace of blazing fire. Then these men were tied up in their trousers, their coats, their caps and their other clothes, and were cast into the midst of the furnace of blazing fire. For this reason, because the king's command was urgent and the furnace had been made extremely hot, the flame of the fire killed those men who carried up Shadrach, Meshach and Abed-nego. But these three men, Shadrach, Meshach and Abed-nego, fell into the midst of the furnace of blazing fire still tied up.

Then Nebuchadnezzar the king was astounded and stood up in haste; he said to his high officials, "Was it not three men we cast bound into the midst of the fire?" They replied to the king, "Certainly, O king." He said, "Look! I see four men loosed and walking about in the midst of the fire without harm, and the appearance of the fourth is like a son of the gods!"

Daniel 3:16-25 NASB

I'm moving you and testing you to trust in Me and to see that I will stand in the fire with you.

-God

"Out Of Sight, Out of Mind"

The Spiritual Visual

This is idea contains two scenarios on how our relationship with God could turn out to be:

Imagine you are on a ship in the sea with accompanying ships and the lighthouse's bright and extensive light is looking to direct the ships to shore and the ships are ready to return home. The closer the ships are to the light house, the more visible the lighthouse becomes to the captain and crew, which in turn has greater visibility and communication signal to hear the needed instructions to dock safely with clarity and accuracy since they are in close proximity. This captain is within the line of sight of the lighthouse. The ships whose communication and navigation equipment is out of date, past due for maintenance and disconnected due to sabotage or negligence is in danger of being beat up by the seas and the winds that come with it thus placing it in great danger of being lost or shipwrecked due to the reckoning of nature. The refusal to stay in sight of and in contact with the lighthouse will increase the inability of the captain to make it safely home if at all. It has happened to where crew members of wrecked ships, who have no way of navigating home, no compass and therefore no way of telling where they are in middle of the sea, have succumb to madness thus succumbing to death: It is unfortunate in this case for those who are Out of Sight,

Out of Mind...

Then you will call upon Me and go and pray to Me, and I will listen to you. And you will seek Me and find Me, when you search for Me with all your heart. I will be found by you, says the Lord, and I will bring you back from your captivity; I will gather you from all the nations and from all the places where I have driven you, says the Lord, and I will bring you to the place from which I cause you to be carried away captive Jeremiah 29:12-14 NKJV

If we are lost at sea in our minds and heart YET remember that there was a time when you were so close to the lighthouse and that the lines of communication and our spiritual compass was in great condition. When God seems far off, we are the ones who have drifted away. And depending upon our choice, we can have Him as near as we possibly can and as much of Him as we so desire. God says we can call upon His name, seek Him with everything we have and we will find Him and He will draw near to us and will return us to His loving presence. Yes, it will be a process but process in this case means progress.

Draw near to God and He will draw near to you. Cleanse your hands, you sinners; and purify your hearts, you double-minded. James 4:8 ESV

God is everywhere. Even in the midst of places where we think he wouldn't be. In the mist of suffering, He is there. When we think we're alone he is there. Even in the times of celebration and joy God celebrates with us. The Lord is always with us. And since He is always with us so is the presence of His Kingdom. As our minds and hearts set themselves on finding help in knowing him the mysteries of Go begins to be unveiled and available. But we must be sure that He is God in our hearts and we must be positive that we desire only to see the kingdom of God then we will truly see and experience all that he desires us to experience. For when the Promised Land was at the forefront of Moses' heart and mind, though He would not show Moses His face, God blessed him to be able to experience His own glory and presence. And believe you me once we are truly in his presence, any and everything this world has to offer will be inadequate to our needs and desires. Imagine this. The King of all kings...God who created everything and breathed life into everyone...Who is everywhere and knows everything and sees all things who has all authority. He says that he will come to our home and knock on our door and to dine with us when we do not come close to being worthy dining with him? He lives in the hearts of those who love him. Give the Lord an open-door policy to fellowship and fill your life fully and completely with Him. Through this, the enemy must either flee or bow.

Behold, I stand at the door and knock; if anyone hears My voice and opens the door, I will come in to him and will dine with him, and he with Me. Revelation 3:20 BLB

The "I Am" Factor

"The tongue can bring death or life; those who love to talk will reap the consequences." Proverbs 18:21 NLT

"And the tongue is a flame of fire. It is a whole world of wickedness, corrupting your entire body. It can set your whole life on fire, for it is set on fire by hell itself." James 3:6 NLT

The Lord's Word is active.

Men have been created in The Lord God's image. (We are created to be a likeness of God, opposed to "being" Him)

So, therefore, though our words are not the final authority, the words we speak are active as well.

Just as God has said, 'You are gods,' I said; 'all of you are children of the Most High.' (Psalm 82:6 NLT) our words hold spiritual weight. They are not the final authority for that belongs to God thank God, yet they are powerful and completely active.

I had an uncle who was highly intelligent who worked as an engineer on space crafts for NASA. Prior to that he flew aircrafts for the army in Desert Storm. Whether or not the former stresses of the war or job requirements and decisions made while in these positions, were the reasons for his severe mental disease, I'm not quite sure of. What I do know is that the weight of his sickness, leading to high blood pressure and anger and resentment of things in life took a toll on him and he eventually succumbed to grips of a massive stroke and then passed away. It was a difficult and unpredictable process to experience externally what he was going through and I remember it all as it was yesterday. When I went through my season in 2010-2011 of stresses, high anxiety, acute psychosis and depression I remember Satan telling me at a particular time, "You're going to be just like your uncle." Though I had a wearied response, I had assured him even as a then infant in the Kingdom of God, "It ain't gonna be me. I am going to be well." I prayed as much as I could. I read and I read and read. I wrote scripture everywhere and after that I wrote them everywhere some more. I kept writing scriptures on anything I could find to make my atmosphere a place to where I'd stumble upon and walk into God's presence and His word at every turn. Even though I did not understand God's word completely (and at most times not at all), the Holy Spirit knew it for me, and He kept me thirsty and hungry for anything and everything from God so that I could stay alive, survive and keep growing. The Lord added His loving and helping hand to my declaration to the Enemy, "I am going to be well." I cannot tell you the exact date and time I left mental illness behind because I was too focused on the footsteps of my Savior Jesus Christ and the eternal and abundant life He promised in His Word.

God has given the words we speak authority and they prove to be powerful, being that we are children of the Most High. So therefore, *Jesus Christ has given us the words to speak and to take hold of* so the power of our words will have greater success according to the will of God, and for our benefit and good. The reason being is that whatever words you speak, from whatever condition your heart may be in, expect that fruit to come into fruition in seed form. And as you continue to speak and intake the spiritual sustenance of the Word and exhortation of God and place these firmly in your atmosphere and plant these seeds into your soil, sowing "life rather than death" from the canals of your heart repeatedly, you will have a full-grown tree with mature roots available for you to indulge in its fruit, that is fulfilling rather than bitter. For as God breathed us to life through our nostrils in Eden, and once more through the last Breath of Christ Jesus on the Cross and the New of His resurrection, so too, our breath can raise to life those who are and that which is dead. Likewise, the lie that Satan breathed on us in Eden for the eternal direction of sin and destruction, we too, with the tongue, can raze soul and space, even our very own, to the grave and Hell itself. The condition of our hope is influenced by the stability of our directed expectation's foundation. Therefore:

1 Peter 1:13 NASB

> "Therefore, prepare your minds for action, keep sober in spirit, fix your hope completely on the grace to be brought to you at the revelation of Jesus Christ."

Lamentations 3:24 NASB

> "The Lord is my portion," says my soul,
> "Therefore I have hope in Him."

Psalms 31:24 NASB

> "Be strong and let your heart take courage, all you who hope in the Lord."

> Let the words you speak be full of power and with the hope of God.

As we speak, we must ask ourselves, "What do I want? Do I want to be healed? Do I want victory?

Do I want to continue where I am, in this place of mental depravity?" And my friends, if we're already aware of the fact that we don't want to be in "this place", we might as well choose life over death and speak into existence what we desire for God to do for us in the mist of this fallen space we are dying in. Being that it already feels like death this is the perfect time to make our vows and petitions to the Lord to open every door that leads to His presence and purposes for your life and we must seek after Him. For vows to the world will surely place you back into a spiritual atmosphere that is barren and lost.

Serious question: If the Lord was willing and able (and He is) to heal you completely from mental illness (no matter the length of the process), would you receive Him as Lord and serve him from this day forward all the days of your life right now as you're reading this? Would you dig in His word to receive the healing you desire to truly have? Would you go to the gates of hell and proclaim and confess Him to the captives with the freedom of God through Christ Jesus has given you? Would you desire the atmosphere of mental depravity on anyone else?

Try the Lord and see that He will do mighty things for you in your life. Pray that the words of your mouth and the mediation of your heart be acceptable in God's sight O Lord my Rock and my Redeemer.

Pray not, Avail not

"Prayvail"

If you're going to worry then don't pray, but if you're going to pray then don't worry. We can't afford to "feel" like praying. We need to "know" we must pray. The devil doesn't "feel" like destroying your life, your marriage or the lives of your children, he "knows" that's what he will do if you are vulnerable enough stray away from praying to our Heavenly Father. The bible doesn't say that Satan "feels" like prowling around like a lion "seldom" seeking here and there who he might devour, it says that he *is seeking* people to kill and devour! In the book of Job chapter one and two, it is written that Satan tells God that he has been going "to and fro on the earth and back and forth on it." To do what you might ask? He had been looking for lives to ruin and destroy. He is the same today as he was then. He knows he wants to kill you.

What I'm about to say is out of love and for the saving of the souls of men yet will be direct, to the point, in-your-face, maybe slightly disrespectful, and very blunt: Get out of your feelings on this one. You better "know" you need to pray. Prayer is the way we fellowship with God and talk to Him about everything that is going on in our lives, everything we have on our heart God wants to know about it. It's not that God doesn't know your heart, but God is looking for our fellowship with Him to be true and unforced. Prayer is also a weapon. Mix prayer with a righteous heart or that is, a heart and mind that believes in Jesus Christ and desires to please God, and you have a prayer that God gives much success. The devil doesn't want us to pray as he so fabricates the idea that our struggles in life are irreparable and hopeless to resolve. This is what wolves and lions do to sheep, because in God's eyes, that's who we are like. We are totally depended on the Father for everything. We can do nothing without what He has provided for us including protection from spiritual harm. These predators, they disrupt the area of the sheep, so they shatter them away from the Shepherd. Then the predator goes in to isolate them and then for the kill. If you are not talking to and in fellowship with God on a daily basis, you are either listening to your flesh on a daily basis or to the lies of Satan.

James 5:16 (KJV) says that the fervent prayers of the righteous availeth much. Which means that they are highly successful and regarded. The reason is because this prayer comes from the heart of someone who desires to please the heart of God. And the thing that brings joy to the heart of God is when we trust Him and believe and receive God's grace and mercy through His son, Jesus Christ. When praying and believing, we take the weight off of ourselves and replace it with the yoke and burden offered by Christ. Jesus taught a parable to show that at all times men and women should pray and not to lose heart. And if the savior of the world says it, then just listen. Come to God in prayer with all things on your mind and heart, believing that He will answer you. And don't leave one rock unturned.

Moments of Meditation

Here are some chapters of scripture to evaluate and see the power of prayer and why we should always not only just pray but pray righteously:

2 Samuel 23

1 Kings 3: 5-15

Matthew 6: 9-13

Authority of the Word...Aloud

Vision of the Valley of Dry Bones

Ezekiel 37: 1-10 NASB

The hand of the LORD was upon me, and He brought me out by the Spirit of the LORD and set me down in the middle of the valley; and it was full of bones. He caused me to pass among them round about, and behold, there were very many on the surface of the valley; and lo, they were very dry. He said to me, "Son of man, can these bones live?" And I answered, "O Lord GOD, You know." Again, He said to me, "Prophesy over these bones and say to them, 'O dry bones, hear the word of the LORD.' "Thus says the Lord GOD to these bones, 'Behold, I will cause breath to enter you that you may come to life. 'I will put sinews on you, make flesh grow back on you, cover you with skin and put breath in you that you may come alive; and you will know that I am the LORD.'" So I prophesied as I was commanded; and as I prophesied, there was a noise, and behold, a rattling; and the bones came together, bone to its bone. And I looked, and behold, sinews were on them, and flesh grew and skin covered them; but there was no breath in them. Then He said to me, "Prophesy to the breath, prophesy, son of man, and say to the breath, 'Thus says the Lord GOD, "Come from the four winds, O breath, and breathe on these slain, that they come to life."'" So I prophesied as He commanded me, and the breath came into them, and they came to life and stood on their feet, an exceedingly great army. Let us breakdown some of these verses of the bible so that we will gain knowledge, wisdom and understanding on speak the word and life out loud in your life on this passage and how we may apply it to our modern day life. The first thing Ezekiel says is that the hand of the Lord was upon me, he was brought out by the Spirit of the Lord, The Holy Spirit, and he was sat down in the middle of the valley. God is always in control. His Word has complete authority over our life...whether we believe in Him or not because His Word does not return to Himself void. Both blessings and curses are active in this world by God. He ponders and scrutinizes all of our ways. He knows everything that we will face in life. Many of us will be called to a valley one way or another. Yet every place we end up in life is intentionally assigned. Just as God has a perfect will for your life, we also have free will. The next words, *"are and it was full of bones, there were many on the surface of the valley and they were very dry."* The valley of life can be a testing, trying, hopeless and spiritually dry place where we thirst but it doesn't seem to be a qualified remedy insight. And there are millions upon millions of people who are without a doubt hopeless and seemingly dried out, and longing to be quenched with something that holds a promise of a full internal, eternal and spiritual restitution. More and more we see that what the world has to offer as a remedy for lack of fulfillment and joy doesn't satisfy in the end. It wears off completely and we are back in the same position we started from, in some cases our situations are made worse if anything.

Then God asks Ezekiel, Can these bones live? Followed with Ezekiel's response, "O Lord, You know." When God asks us a question pertaining to our lives or life in general, He already knows the answer. Instead, the faith and belief in the mind and heart of a person is revealed and what that faith has been placed in. Ezekiel's response is translated

Then the drumroll comes in and God says to Ezekiel, "Prophesy over these bones and say to them, hear the word of the Lord, and again, Behold, I will cause breath to enter you that you may come to life... and put breath in you that you may come alive...; and you will know that I am the LORD. Lastly, Ezekiel says, "So I prophesied as He commanded me, and the breath came into them, and they came to life and stood on their feet, an exceedingly great army. Just as the dry bones in the valley in Ezekiel, when we are in the valley of life, we must prophesy and speak the word of God and His commands out loud for ourselves to hear what God is speaking to us and edifying our inward being. If we can read it and listen it through any bible application simultaneously. This is so that the breath of life and strengthening of our bones will be given to us and renewed in us as well. Then we too are exceedingly great in the army of the Lord, hearing the power needed to overthrow the power of the enemy who had been inwardly working against us to bring us to incapacity.

The "God" Standard

Many times when we are striving after the heart of God and seeking Him and His presence for healing in our mental health, true peace, and growth in our inner being, we can also be in the presence of those who may not have, per se, an interest in going that far with their relationship with God. They may have normalized strife and foolishness in their own life. They are just comfortable where they are. We shouldn't of course judge them for that decision because they have the free will to make choices in life.

That's their standard. But through the cross at Calvary, Jesus Christ has granted to us the freedom to draw near to God's presence as close as we can. We have been granted full 24-hour access to the well that holds the Living Water and we can quench and nourish ourselves as much as we like without reservation. We can come to the throne of grace at anytime from anywhere as much as we either need to or have the pleasure in doing so. We can go deeper with our Heavenly Father and it only depends on how far we want to go. And if others aren't ready for that journey, that's ok. If you are being called to take that journey, then you go. In Genesis 12: 1-7 The Lord God calls out to Abram (later he is called "Abraham") and tells him to leave his country, his relatives, and his father's house and start heading towards the land that The Lord wanted going to show him. Then God explained to Abram how He was going to cause him to be the father of a great nation and He would make him famous. The Lord told Abram that he would be a blessing to others and that God would bless those who blessed him and curse those who cursed him, and all the families on the earth would be blessed through him. And Abram left all that he had known behind as the Lord had instructed him – and his nephew Lot went with him. Even Lot knew that Abram's future was too good to not follow in his footsteps. See Abram's family was happy where they were, for they were happy worshipping the idols of the land. But the Lord called Abram I believe because chapter 12 and 13 shows that Abram would listen to God and follow every instruction the Lord called him to obey. God knows the desires of our hearts and I believe that God knew Abram wanted more for himself. Abram may not have known where the Lord was leading him, but he knew that the desires in the hearts of his country, family and father's house was leading him to a place called, "Nowhere." The Holy Spirit grants it, and God calls us to come and we will find pleasure in our decision to draw closer to Him. God's promise to us is that we will find ourselves and who we are only in Him through Christ and find pleasure and purpose in the place He's leading us to. The Lord will give us His grace and peace when we seek and pursue Him to know Him. There is more to obtain in Christ Jesus. There's more! There's more for you – if you want it. Abram desired a standard that was much greater than the standards offered by his home country and the Lord called Abram to offer him an opportunity of a lifetime, literally from one generation to generations to come. God offered him a standard that was beyond his ability to understand or comprehend. In Genesis 15:5, The Lord told Abram to look up at the heavens and the stars in the night sky and count them if he could. Then He said that the number of stars in the sky is a representation of the number of Abram's future descendants. Just as the stars are too numerous to count, the blessings of God are likewise. We'll call this the "God Standard".

    The Bible says that Enoch walked with God, and he was not for the Lord took him. What does the Bible mean that "he was not"? Did Enoch walk so close with God that he no longer fit in with anyone around him? Was he no longer any earthly good? We don't know for sure. But what we do know is that there is One who is much greater than Enoch in every way, and He sets the standard in how we should follow and walk with God. And we can have as much of Him as we like. Jesus is the Cornerstone in which we set the foundation to build our stronghold through the power of the

Holy Spirit to dwell in, to be pleasing to God and to receive His covering around us. The God Standard we strive towards hold the fruits of the Spirit. These fruits would be: Love, joy, peace, forbearance (patience), kindness, goodness, faithfulness, gentleness and self-control. And the more we grow in the knowledge of God and Christ Jesus our Lord, in 2 Peter 1:2-4 it says that, "grace and peace is multiplied to us". It then says that we will be able to, not imagine but actually with our own eyes, see and be a witness to God's divine power supplied to us for the purposes of being made alive with Christ's eternal indwelling and heavenly perspective. Also, we will grow in the godliness that Christ died for us to acquire. The closer we draw to God through Christ, the more apparent the fruits of the Spirit become. The more apparent they are, knowing how to know the atmosphere of God, the more "addictive" He and His Word and presence becomes. The testing and trials might become tougher, sometimes a little longer, the distractions that try and steer you away from reading His word increase, but none the less, the more equipped we become, having every available resource of heaven to break chains and overcome the burdened mindset. For Christ is He and His presence is where, not what, mankind has truly been searching for, which is eternal life and His eternal living within our earthly bodies and on Earth around us. But we are failed when we attempt to acquire the atmosphere of God through the fabricated and false vices of the flesh and Satan, which is nowhere near in comparison to the peace of and through Jesus Christ, the Redeemer. So what happens when, as we desire to draw near to God, mental healing, inner restitution, freedom from strife, a pure mind and heart and everything else we need to come alive, it is evaluated that His presence is not the apparent standard for those individuals looking to interlock themselves and do life with you? We do not suppose, since we now desire more of God and His promises, that we are now better than anyone. Nor should we allow anyone to make us feel guilty or like we are acting "Holier Than Thou" for "moving on or forward into our promise". We can continue and still love those who aren't ready to go further with you into the calling of God. In some cases there are people close to us who see what God is doing or wants to do in your life like Lot and say okay I'm willing to good with you. They may only be able to go so far but then they go their separate way and you yours so as to understand that you have an assigned individual purpose and calling from the Lord yourself, and they themselves. We continue to pray for their hearts that they too answer and are mighty in the call of God. It could be family, friends, or whoever we are praying for and encouraging to God, but we aren't responsible to answer the call belonging to someone else nor should you allow yourself to "stay" where they are if God is calling you to a new land. We must, however, make a wise determination and a decision, for the health, nurturing and growth of our inward self and that which God has entrusted us to tend to, as to what we want to live with…and what we can live without.

"God-stile Takeover"

During my battle against mental illness, I would make every effort to drive to church in Gardena, CA in 2010-2011. I remember actually having an anxiety episode while there at the church. I actually drove to church already anxious. When I got there I sought much needed prayer because I was struggling. They prayed for me and still had to call the ambulance and once again I was admitted to the hospital but after that the hospital released me that same day. After they released me I was just walking around area in a daze. I found a place to sit and I was just starring off in the days into nowhere. Then a voice said to me, "Go back to the church." I was still out of it and was going back and forth whether or not to make that trek because my mind was quite foggy. I stopped to eat something at a fast food restaurant but it felt like after I received what I ordered I looked down at my food and it was gone nor did I feel like I ate anything. Yes, my mental state reached a point where I was medically diagnosed with acute psychosis. The mind gets to a point where you have no sense of time, direction, and awareness. Many times I would be anxious due to having "memory loses and time lapses in memory-you could have found yourself doing some things and thinking in ways that are simply obscure. I've walked around at night in the park, I would just stand outside of my door and stare off into the distance. I would conjure up "worlds" in my mind as if reality wasn't worth living in. When you come to your senses, you'll have this, "What am I doing right now?" moments. It could be daytime when you then experience this sort of clouded mindset, then you come back to your senses and then you realize that three or four hours pass have passed by, which could turn your day into night if it happens at a particular time of day. Moving along, I know there was a spiritual struggle for me because I was in an area down in Gardena that was somewhat unfamiliar with nor would I consider it a safe to just be walking around in with nowhere to go. So I just started walking back to the church. But then on the way back, I stopped at another fast food place to get a cup of water because it was hot that day, especially for this long walk back to the church. But I walked anyways. I walked and walked. The church was about a mile or so away from the hospital. Along the way a little breeze hit my face that was much needed. The sun was subsiding as well so that helped. I had finally made it back to church and I found that my keys were locked in the church office the security guard told me. So I asked the security guard if someone he knew could give me a ride home back to Anaheim. As he was asking around a guy around the age of 30 or so offered to help me out. He was pretty much going the same direction so it all worked out. Well, when I got in the car we talked and we ended up praying for one another. It was a blessing that I made it back to the church because I got back when night service had well past ended. But I made it back for this gentleman, who God ordained a ride home and who was going through some things in his life as well, to prophesy over me. I'm not going to tell you what he prophesied. All I will tell you for now is that I received it.

The Take Over

One day I was praying while driving back from church and I asked God for two things: I wanted a church close to where I lived in Anaheim and I wanted to fully understand the scriptures and what was being preached. I wanted more because I was starving spiritually. So I Googled some churches around the Orange County area that I ended up visiting and they were ok. But how I ended up finding a church is by applying for Food Stamps. I know right? Food Stamps. We have our way of finding a church…and then God has His way of finding us one. But anyways, I was applying for assistance and come to find out that I made too much money to qualify…Didn't know $350.00 after taxes a week in 2010 and no kids at the time was too much money but anyways, moving right along. So the advisor recommended I try and visit one of the churches on their list that offered food donations to those who needed it. So I went to go pick up food on a Saturday and ended up picking up a church home in the process. So one Sunday morning during church service, the senior pastor mentioned that in the foyer there were bible study booklets with DVD's for free and, yes, I did say FREE that he had designed and put together for new believers to go through and grow in their faith and walk with Jesus Christ. I took everything! I took all four parts of the bible study with their additional DVD's that he prepared that same day right after service. Every chance I had and everyday throughout the week I began to devour God's Word on a daily basis. To be honest, I'm not trying to sound like super bible man, but studying God's word became a hobby to me. The television stayed off. The music I listen to changed. My spirit began to become quiet. My atmosphere began to be different. I began to find places to sit with God. I had the mindset to talk to God and have Him nurture me after receiving Him. I became more and surer of my eternal life from God through Christ Jesus who loves me and died to clear me from the guilt and condemnation of my sins. I grew in the knowledge of who He is and what He says verses what the devil was telling me. I was forgiven. I still am. I would stumble here and there but at least I was now headed in the right direction. His peace began to rest in me. The Holy Spirit began to teach me and He truly began to remind me of His word.

The Holy Spirt Speaks

I was curious to know more about Jesus so I would listen to YouTube pastors at times but I ended up coming across as a young Christian a YouTube channel by a Muslim that was titled, "10 Reason Why Jesus Is Not God". And I'm looking at this post intrigued so I click it of course because that's what you do when you get on YouTube, everything is interesting. But as I was listening to the Muslim, I learned that he used to profess Christianity and used to be a youth bible teacher so I guess that pushed for his so–called credibility on bible knowledge. And one of the main claims he made about Jesus not being God is because He never said that He was God verbatim.

Then something happened.

A voice says to me these words: "Therefore God, Your God." That's all I received. I became curious. I paused the video and I did what any curious person would do looking for clarity... and I Googled the phrase and this passage came up:

But about the Son he says,

> "Your throne, O God, will last for ever and ever; a scepter of justice will be the scepter of your kingdom.
>
> You have loved righteousness and hated wickedness;
>
> _Therefore God, your God_, has set you above your companions by anointing you with the oil of joy."

He also says,

> "In the beginning, Lord, you laid the foundations of the earth, and the heavens are the work of your hands.

Hebrews 1:8-10 NIV

Wow...

The Muslim was caught in what we call a half-truth. The devil used them in the Garden of Eden. He uses them all the time. The truth is this: Jesus didn't have to call Himself God and Lord word for word because, according to this passage of scripture, God does it for Him. That's a hostile takeover but by the teaching of the Holy Spirit. He completely snatched back to Himself my attention and curious heart from wavering and doubting Him as a new Christian. That's a God-stile Takeover. From that moment, God taught me that whatever information I receive in this world, make sure and see whether or not He, The Holy Spirit, has already co-signed on it in the Bible. I now understood what others meant about the sound of His still small voice...

"Focus and Boundaries"

"Religion that is pure and good before God the Father is to help children who have no parents and to care for women whose husbands have died who have troubles. Pure religion is also to keep yourself clean from the sinful things of the world" James 1:27 NLV

There are two parts in this chapter that I will be addressing so bear with me.

The Focus

Orphans had no parents to care for them or physical guardians to protect them from physical harm and teach them God's laws and how to go about in life. Their lives remained at stake.

Wives in these times were completely depended on their husbands to provide for them and to protect them. If a woman became a widow, her life could have been in danger as well, whether through homelessness, hunger, or physical harm. In scripture, we know that God is our Heavenly Father. We also know God the Son, Christ Jesus to be "The Bridegroom" or the husband and head of God's family, the church. Can we imagine seeing wives in harm's way and children suffering because either the husband is not alive to provide or the father is not there to protect, teach and guide? It simply breaks the heart of God being that these are His first responsibilities towards us- because He is the Father in Heaven and Christ Jesus is the Bridegroom or husband of the family of God. And since these responsibilities are covered by the true essence of His character, care for the orphan and widow is considered "pure and undefiled religion". It was considered real "religion" (I prefer the word, "relationship") and reverence and love for God because this would prove that you knew and understood who God is, what He does and what He's done and is doing for you. Therefore, care for those in this situation was the very first priority for those who had a true heart for God and wanted to serve Him.

Any attention given to things that overlooked these two top priorities or that focused on other false "religious" innuendos like what you wore or your "religious prestige", where you worshipped God, how many times you washed your hands, how you prayed in public was by far irrelevant nor did it prove spiritual purity and relationship with God. Not only that, blessing and loving God and cursing others and gossiping about people with the same tongue is like saying that I want to have a healthier diet and live a healthy life but never having any intention of cutting food with tons of sugar and salt form my diet.

Jesus told the woman at the well that it didn't matter where she prayed. Whether she prayed in Jerusalem or on the mountain, worshipping God in Spirit and truth is what matters the most. The condition of the heart while worshipping God and focusing on your calling by God and existence is the priority.

My main questions are these: What's are the pure and undefiled religions that God has assigned to you? And what are the polluting and distracting things (and people) surrounding your life? What and where has God called you to set boundaries in your life so that your mind and spirit can grow healthy and stay correct and on point so that you can focus on your P.U.R. (pure and undefiled religion)?

Your Boundaries

Granted, care for widows and orphans is still important, yet this whole world has gotten more and more off balance and dim that distress is everywhere and around every corner. Maybe you're the one that the Lord has delivered from or has led through something difficult or a season in life that many in the world are still suffering from and sending the distress signal. They are waiting for you. They are waiting for you to say "yes" to your purpose and "no" to entertaining anything that is purposeless and outside of God's calling for your life. In February 2019, the Lord blessed me to facilitate and teach the Word of God for a well-known non-profit to men whom, I would soon discover, The Lord was calling to a greater depth in Him. When I went through the necessary steps and processes to be approved to volunteer there to teach, a Major for the non-profit, who gave me the approval to teach, looked me in the eyes and said, "I believe you are the one whom The Lord has sent to teach these men." Another said, "welcome aboard! We've been praying for and waiting for you!" Every attack came from everywhere by the enemy for seven months prior to teaching, but focusing on the approval, strength and timing of the Lord and setting boundaries for my life ,for the sake of God's men, to whom He was sending me to teach set my footing for me to answer the call. You have to create boundaries for yourself and keep others from hounding them with everything that is opposite to God's presence and focus for you. Sometimes it's not that what people are inviting you to or drawing to you is ungodly or bad, it's just that every person needs a substantial amount of time to self-care and most importantly Sabbath with Jesus Christ and our Heavenly Father. Having boundaries from people or things interfering with your Hymostphere, bringing godless behavior or focus, worldly wisdom, distractions from your needs and "busyness", will put you on a road to achieve both physical and spiritual health and balance in life. But you must be intentional in filling that "empty" space with God things. That may be spending time in His Word, running, or hiking in nature, writing that Spirit-inspired book or blog, cleaning your living space, creating art, listening to worship music and praying, or something you enjoy doing that you can also dedicate it as time with God that doesn't oppose the peace of God and invite the atmosphere that we are moving away from. BUT YOU MUST have space and time to do YOU. Just know, as you spend time with God, you will discover "you" through His eyes in His presence. And that's the real you. For our plans, thoughts and knowledge we have for and of ourselves are extraordinarily minimal to the thoughts, plans and love God has for us to know and experience. Note that you barely have to tell people that you're withdrawing from them. Rather, by simply drawing near to God through Christ Jesus will either, to others, be appealing and convincing or "appalling" and "condemning" (which is conviction of the Spirit under fire). And you will notice, the more you stay overflowed with God's Spirit and control your boundaries the more you will have to give when the time comes to give, and spiritually speaking, the less appealing you'll be with those not seeking God's Spirit. Think of a water dam. If the barrier stops the flood then the water just sits. If it lowers down the reserves behind the wall decrease. If they stay open or broken down then the dam has no water reserves to supply the area from which it came and where the water is headed will probably flood a land not able to receive it. Then you will began to thirst as well while those you are watering misuse or disregard the "fulfillments" God has given you. Your reserves are to be used by God and a testimony for others to draw near to God and Christ Jesus to receive the same reserves in full for themselves.

Guard Your Temple

When it was almost time for the Jewish Passover, Jesus went up to Jerusalem. In the temple courts he found people selling cattle, sheep and doves, and others sitting at tables exchanging money. So he made a whip out of cords, and drove all from the temple courts, both sheep and cattle; he scattered the coins of the money changers and overturned their tables. To those who sold doves he said, "Get these out of here! Stop turning my Father's house into a market!" His disciples remembered that it is written: "Zeal for your house will consume me." The Jews then responded to him, "What sign can you show us to prove your authority to do all this?" Jesus answered them, "Destroy this temple, and I will raise it again in three days." They replied, "It has taken forty-six years to build this temple, and you are going to raise it in three days?" But the temple he had spoken of was his body. After he was raised from the dead, his disciples recalled what he had said. Then they believed the scripture and the words that Jesus had spoken.

John 2: 12- 22 NIV

Your body, mind and spirit was entrusted to you by God. The Creator of the Universe. By no means should we resist evil people as Jesus Christ commands but you should never linger on doorsteps where you've kicked dust off of your shoes due to others rejection of the Gospel. For if you linger there, the dust that is to be a witness against that home who've rejected the Gospel will also be a witness against you and your home. We are to keep it moving.

The mind and heart that has received the presence and power of Christ through the Holy Spirit should not become entangled with the mind and heart(s) that has not, especially while in mental turmoil. This helps keep us under the covering of God's healing and peace and protecting us from the hindrance of God's work in our lives.

When your "new home" meaning your inner person that Jesus Christ is now living in, is being taken advantage of, not stewarded properly, or even misused, humbly make your whip out of cords (spiritually) and start swinging and flipping tables, not out of spite but out of love and obedience to God and His presence in your atmosphere. And yes, that also means the-stepping- away from toxic relationships and people. Because at the end of the day, you're the only person that's going to deal with your inner sanity after being ransacked by the insanity, mental, spiritual and emotional negligence, intentional ignorance and foolishness of others. No offense.

A Shield Around You

In the days of Abram (Abraham), Lot, when parting ways from Abram because both of their families were too numerous to dwell in the same place together, took all that he had and settled on the outskirts of Sodom and Gomorrah. Lot was a righteous man, yet later in the Book of Genesis, we find that Lot's family went from living on the outskirts of these cities to moving inside of Sodom. Instead of moving forward and finding another place to dwell away from Sodom, the actions and practices of the city became less and less of a godly offense to Lot to the point where the Sodom now became the "status quo". Lot knew the wickedness that dwelt in Sodom yet he and his family lingered at their doorsteps until the city's influences lured them in, causing the righteous to "coexist" with unrighteousness. God eventually rescued Lot from the destruction of Sodom and Gomorrah, but turned Lot's wife into a pillar of salt because of the desires of her heart longing to remain there- in a lifestyle that was on the verge of God's judgement. Both the rescuing of Lot from these cities and the unfortunate repercussions of his wife looking back, was the hand of God guarding and protecting the righteous temples that belonged to Him. Through Christ Jesus, we must be mindful of the spiritual grounds we are treading on and the influences around us so that we are not lingering in the wrong places, relationships, attitudes and ambitions to where we too begin to coexist with things that aren't bringing us closer to Jesus and the healing and miracles He wants to do in our lives. The temple during the Jewish Passover looked righteous and holy from the outside and through the ignorant eyes and understanding of those who were innocently looking to sacrifice and give honor and praise to God. Yet when Jesus walked in the house that originally belongs to God, evaluations, leading to exhortations and cleansing as well as corrections and rebuke had to take place. The zeal for God, the Holy Spirit must be on and in your spiritual home to be in your physical home. You must guard *your* temple of God. Either that or Satan and the vices of the flesh will sift you like wheat. For God's temple on earth must move, through His Spirit, towards resembling His temple in heaven.

We spend years of our life either building ourselves to "look" like a particular manner all of our lives and we've been built by someone else's sinful actions, negligence or false wisdom leading us to being unfulfilled in life. The hopelessness we've endured causes us to carry a worn down version of our mentality no matter how hard we try to move forward or higher in our own strength. This attracts mental health issues or a spiritual draining and disrupts our so-called peace. The reason being is that we are trying to use the power of the world to correct the brokenness of our world. And if the world is broken then what power does it really have? How much is its wisdom and love really worth? Concerning this world, what we are told would bring us peace, joy and power, and success, apart from Jesus Christ, is a lie from the spirit of the world and the flesh. Yet, when Jesus comes into our heart and lives, His love and power challenges and penetrates our "strong foundations" in the world, razes them to the core and if we are humble enough, rebuilds our earthly temple to true life and purpose. For anything: any peace, any joy and happiness, or hope or future, any power or might, any knowledge or wisdom, any love not built on the foundation of Jesus Christ is sure to fall and fail. Yet anything and everything that is being rebuilt by God is sure to stand. That includes your heart and mind.

Don't copy the behavior and customs of this world, but let God transform you into a new person by changing the way you think. Then you will learn to know God's will for you, which is good and pleasing and perfect.

Romans 12:2 NLT

Stand guard over your temple for the glory of God.

"The Hidden Scroll in the Dead Sea"

Talk.
I mean, just talk.
I reiterate: Talk.
If you don't like something, then say it.
Call it out.
Speak up.

A little knowledge about The Dead Sea: Scrolls held thousands of words and the reason why the Dead Sea is full of, well, dead things is because there is one inlet into the sea but no outlet. Sort of like a cul-de-sac. So everything builds up and sits and eventually festers. The excessive amount of salt and dead fish grows to a point where the water becomes too polluted to drink or sustain life.

You need an outlet.

The issues and concerns of life will happen with no question. But if you don't have a place, person or people you can confide in and simply share your heart with then your inner self will eventually fester and become polluted. Not only will we pollute ourselves but we will pollute every relationship we're involved in, it will spill over into our jobs, or home life, and it will continue to be an interference to normal life. Heart attack, stroke, heart disease, cancers caused by stress and mental illness all come to fruition because we don't talk and release what's bothering or eating us up inside. If we want to go a little deeper, we don't like to talk to God about the things that are eating us up inside - nor do we like to confess things before God either because we may not believe He hears us, sees us or cares for us. But these conversations and confessions to God, as well as to godly and wise men and women, lead to not only the forgiveness of God, but also to the receiving of direction, instruction and peace from God, being that sometimes the things that are weighing us down and bothering us really have nothing to do with us being in the wrong. Sometimes it's just us being in the world. I still have to even remind myself to talk, share, and confess, both to God and men about the issues that I have. But as we share, we have to ensure that we are available to receive *and* apply *fresh water* to purify and cleanse us- which comes by godly wisdom and counselors and by the Word of God- and not just releasing to simply dump your baggage on someone. Personally, sometimes I still struggle with weakness disguised as my own false meekness and this thinking that I have things under control and that I don't need to share what's on my heart. Other times I feel like I don't want to talk about issues I have in my marriage or fatherly relationships in life because I "don't want conflict" or "I just want to keep the peace with the next person and make everyone happy." Peace comes at a price. But it's a price worth paying because when we talk and open up wisely yet honestly, the truth sets us free. And we receive honest wisdom for us to in turn apply to our lives. Having peace sometimes means going to the front line and fighting in the trenches to take hold of it. That's why I think I've heard people say, "Speak your peace, buddy." Simply because it sets us free.

You Are What You Eat

One of the most serious vices that had overtaken me at a young age was pornography. The videos were semi-freely available for me to indulge in my home as a teenager and the continual consumption of this material began to shape and mold my thinking for the worst, as I sunk deep into self-worthlessness and a high altitude of lust. I began to believe that my flesh and body was to only be used for the purposes of pleasing and self-pleasure through sexual immorality. This consumption took place year after year all the way up until my mid-20s. My mind had been so influenced by pornography that by this time anytime I would look at a woman or myself all I could think of was "object of sex." Not that this is someone's daughter or mother, not that this is someone's niece not even of myself could I see more than someone who could give and lusted for physical pleasure. I couldn't imagine what my mother or grandmother might've thought about my life style. I could have cared less if people loved me, what others would have thought but most importantly I couldn't even comprehend or even care what or how much God thought of me. And for this reason what I ate is what I became. Vile, vicious, angry, lustful, proud, seductive only caring about what my body needed to feel alive. But I was worse than the corpses in the graveyard: the living dead. And I still remember one day... I remember how the waiting room looked, I remember how the clerk looked at me when I paid the money. The signs leading to this clinic were burned into my brain. I had every opportunity to walk away but I didn't. I had a fear of being criticized and a fear of feeling that I've messed up my life. I had a fear of not being able to take care for a child. I thought that I could just cover it up. In my mind, I said to myself, "No one is going to know. I did this in "secret" so I should just move on with my life. It will go away eventually." I was taught about God. I believed in God. But that doesn't mean anything given the truth that demons believe in God as well. And they are terrified of God's judgment that waiting for them for their disobedience. And after I committed this horrible sin, fear and "shutter" built up in my bones of God's punishment. And I ran for nine years. I even moved to a different state to get away from "it". But both the conviction and condemnation stood by waiting for me to come down from my high of being in a "new and exciting place", being full of "optimism" for the possibilities available to me in a new state. But I would soon enough hit a wall. The wall of stagnancy, senseless direction and spiritual blindness. Then those fears joined in with the previous and it began to be manifested in my body. High-blood pressure, anxiety and panic attacks, stress and sleepless nights, depression and hopelessness from foreseeing an empty and lonely future, which added more fear, which caused me to break and fall apart. I could no longer function properly as an everyday citizen. There were days where I wouldn't show up to work, nor did I bother to call my employer. I just wanted to sleep all day hoping that when I woke up everything would be normal. Yet, I was afraid when I laid down to sleep for fear of death while sleeping for the consequences of my sins and actions. I thought that "it" would just "go away" but all I did was sow a seed that would lead me towards self-condemnation. Yet I tried to "hide it" and run from the thoughts for nearly a decade without confessing it to God. It's because at the time, I didn't believe God would forgive me. Other times I figured that God already knew about my sin and so it wasn't any need to address it. There was a heart issue that I had that was in need of spiritual repair. Believing that God hears and answers the prayers from now and even of the generations past, God in His response, stepped in. Thankfully. By this time my actions were tearing me up and I was full of brokenness inside. That's the place where God did some of His best work in me: when I was completely broken and had finally Surrendered *completely*. I would have panic and anxiety attacks that were so forceful, I could feel them increasing in strength as they were happening. Panic attacks normally come out of nowhere. But I knew when these where coming and they were horrible. I tried my best to prosper at my job and using my talents and gifts to take my mind off of them, but I was left with nothing but confusion in my thinking, not having a clue of who I was or where I was going in life. I had no idea what was going on. And some or most days I wasn't even mentally present- because of psychosis and psychotic episodes. Other days, I was stricken and paralyzed by fear and being paranoid and anxious of the next possible panic attack. I would call the ambulance so many times thinking I was dying and after a while they decided to admit me to the mental hospital. I eventually had to be prescribed psychiatric medicine. But I felt like if I had to take medication, I personally didn't want it to be forever. I soon found out personally that there is a huge difference between walking with and following Jesus verses just being raised in a Christian home. I had to receive Jesus Christ as Lord over my life by the choice given to *me* by God. I couldn't (and we won't) make it to heaven on the basis of someone else's faith and relationship with Christ. And even in the midst of my mental illness and episodes, God opened up for me "clear windows of opportunity" in my mind and in my heart *to make a decision.* Moving to a different place was not enough. Being "good" from now on doesn't suffice. The sin needed to be addressed. But better now than later. God has a way of chiseling and the know how to use a jack hammer and other tools to draw out your obedience and praise, lest your heart is settled in rebellion against Him. On the outside I looked normal but mental illness for me was literally internal *suffering and suffocating.* I did not *need* to live defeated, both in this life and eternally. Quite frankly, I no longer wanted to either. You see, my grandmother and mother made sure I was in church from a youth. While in church, the pastors, deacons and elders always sang these Southern-style hymns that sounded like groans and humming. And for the life of me I had absolutely no idea what any of them were saying nor could I understand what these hymns meant …*until I was in my valley.* And let me tell *you* that every single one of those hymns and hums, while in the valley, that I could remember as a youth came out freely and God-willingly. They didn't just come out though, but I *projected them thangs*' out loud, in the hospital and psych ward, no matter who was around. Let just say I received Jesus Christ as Lord and Savior but I remained in this valley atmosphere. The seed of redemption and sanctification had been planted through faith. God's reason for leaving me here? In my current understanding, back then I knew nothing of God. I had to learn how to walk and trust in Him alone and follow Jesus. The Psalmist David didn't say even though I stand, sit or sleep through the valley. He said even though I *walk through* the valley. God trained and still is training me through and by His word in righteousness and my fingers for the battles in the valleys to come. He had work for me to do and I was all in. I discovered that there was nothing else in life worthy of being considered worth anything - only Jesus and me knowing Him more. My old self left me broken and if I allowed it to, it would have dragged me to the pit of hell. I was already on the brink of self-destruction or at least it seemed that way. I did not want to be in the atmosphere of the valley any longer. So I sat daily in the presence of God and His Word.

I would soon come across a passage of Proverbs where Solomon wrote,

"He that covereth his sins shall not prosper: but whoso confesseth and forsaketh them shall have mercy. "Proverbs 28:13 KJV

As I was thinking and writing this chapter, this passage of scripture came to mind:

"All Scripture is inspired by God and profitable for teaching, for reproof, for correction, for training in righteousness; so that the man of God may be adequate, equipped for every good work."

2 Timothy 3:17 NASB

The scriptures here is the Law of God, and now the Bible, is the type of media used in those days to inquire of the Lord's instruction but not all media is inspired by God. Pornography is not God-breathed and was only useful in the attempts to destroy my soul. There are all kinds of television shows, films, and social media outlets that are used irresponsibly that promotes hurtful stereotypes, racism, sexism, pride and coveting hearts, lust, greed and selfish ambition. When our eyes are captured by visual representations of "entertaining" yet depraved creative material, those who have consumed this food have been left angry and misinformed due to false representation of their culture and way of life creating generational foundations of premeditated ignorance, cruel barriers, superstitions and divisions based on lies and assumptions. Some forms of media has no substance whatsoever. Some are rather loving the divisions it causes and love "thriving" from them. Sometimes our flesh is tempted by media to get tangled in comparison traps and covet the lives of fake characters they see on television and on the front of magazines appearing to be doing "better than you." In turn the consumer finds themselves depressed and saddened because the person in the social media post "has everything to smile about in their life" making you feel as if your life will never be "that good". And it's not that it's bad it just paints one picture and moment of their life where they finally received a moment to smile or laugh. It doesn't tell everything. This is why it's important to take into consideration first what God says about us. We have to use God's media in order determine if what we are consuming on a daily basis is preparing us for every good work God has us for. We have to ask ourselves: Is what I'm consuming from my daily media appetite lining my mind up with the will of God and what He's trying to do in my life? And also we can take into consideration that even though a liberty may not necessarily lead to death, it doesn't mean that it will lead you to life either. There are some liberties and pursuits that prove to be a waste of time and promote a stagnant life. This would leave the person whom God is trying to work miracles through spiritually and purposefully immobilized.

"And the disciples came to the other side of the sea, but they had forgotten to bring any bread. And Jesus said to them, "Watch out and beware of the leaven of the Pharisees and Sadducees." Then they understood that He did not say to beware of the leaven of bread, but of the teaching of the Pharisees and Sadducees."

Matthew 16:5-6, 12 NASB.

Sadducees in Jesus' day were known to disregard some truths of God's Word such as the resurrection of the Messiah if it couldn't be examined literally in the scriptures. And Jesus called the Pharisees a brood of vipers and that they had the ability to make someone twice the son of hell than they were. And it was all hidden behind the desires of the hearts of men and behind that look of power, abundance, and beauty. One of the main reasons Jesus' word was not regarded well because of his outward appearance and His birthplace (a lightbulb for us who "love" Jesus but disregard the wisdom and knowledge of those who lack the modern-day appearance of "prestige").

There's Nothing New Under The Sun.

Music is another tool used by Satan to get us to say certain things and think certain ways we wouldn't even come close to consider thinking or saying without the infectious yet distracting vibe of a nice rhythm. It's a *Job tactic*. Yet, instead of pain, Satan will also use the pleasures of the flesh. But in the Book of Job, Satan bet God that he could get Job to curse Him to His face. Satan's vice for tempting Job to curse God, since he was very wealthy, was to attack and take away all the possessions, and when that didn't entice Job to curse God, it is written Satan told God that Job would curse Him if he (Satan) was allowed to attack Job's health. Job's appearance and health condition was so bad that his wife decided to chime in with her two cents. Job's wife's "exhortation" to Job is telling of the repercussions and consequences for cursing God when she tempted Job to just "curse God and die" because his body was in such horrible shape leaving him in much despair. Can you imagine your spouse, the one who's supposed to be there for you through better or worse, encouraging you to do whatever you have to do to die?

Yep, and that's probably the reason why that was the last time we hear about her in the remaining parts of the book.

Yes, Satan will use even your spouse, if they're vulnerable enough, to get you to eternally put your food in your mouth. Words matter. Word's do far more damage than sticks and stones because they are spiritual. Our mouth was given power by God. When you think of someone being a devil's advocate, you think of lawyers. Because in cases that revolve around life and death, the lawyers are the one's trained to be on constant lookout for words and information that incriminate and discredit the opposition in order to help their firm win the case. Satan knows we won't say certain things to God's face like curse Him with a conscious mind, or speak mindless words into existence, unless there lies within that person a certain amount ignorance, spiritual immaturity or sheer disregard for God. So Satan reached back into His bag of skills, which is music. If the devil wants to convince you to say something vile to God, over the life of someone else or even yourself, he'll just put a dope beat to it. He'll hide it behind the beautiful sound of strings and piano, the jamming and subtle strum of guitar strings, and behind a hardened heart and voice that can masterful strike any note. Jesus said it's not what goes into a man that defiles Him but what comes out of him. In this passage, Jesus makes it clear that physical food doesn't defile a person but what is spiritually stored in our heart will eventually come out of our mouth and defile a person in every way. Media that encourage certain life styles, worldly ideologies and practices that are intentionally in opposition to God's word are in high production. I noticed that the world wants less to do with God and His redeeming Holy Spirit, and more with mediums and psychics. Though they may have knowledge they do not compare or even come close to the knowledge and wisdom of Christ Jesus. And since God's word speaks against the counsel of mediums, psychics and soothsayers, the information they offer is not from God. For demons have higher knowledge and they *know* that Jesus is the Son of God. But just because they know this does not mean that they are *of or from* Jesus. It's just information to them. It does not mean that they love Him or speak with pure motives. Satan tempted Jesus with His own word, but maligning the word of God to The Word of God in order to "trick" the Son of God. Therefore, just because some knowledge is revealed to us from the *heavenly places* does not mean that the source of that knowledge is pure. Angels of God only declare and obey the commands and truth of God and His word. Yet, it is information that needs to be lined up with the complete truth of God's word that we unveil the heart of the source. Since we, our flesh, tend to desire more of something that may seem appealing, we can find ourselves being lead on a string by a bit of information and then finding ourselves entangled with something or someone who is godless and unholy in heart. A great question to ask yourself when presented with "information" is, "Why are you telling me this?" or "Why is this being shared with me?" "Is it truth?" Our life experiences can also defile us. I covered this issue in a previous chapter but let me reiterate, we can't allow ourselves to be someone else's trash can. A person has to be able to process and burn their own trash, if it's trash to them in the first place. The saying goes "One man's trash is another man's treasure." Well, that's not the case in the spiritual and godly realm. One man's trash is another man's burden. That's where Jesus Christ comes in. All spiritual claims must be directed to Jesus Christ. He's the one who can relate to us in every way. If we are to receive anything to move towards healing of mind, it must be the daily consumption of the Bread of Life and Living Water- The Word of God, Jesus Christ.

Rest

I remember nights where I was so full of anxiety for fear that I would have a panic attack in my sleep that I could not close my eyes to rest. So I laid in my bed hoping and trying to pray myself to sleep. On a similar occasion I decided to read the bible until I fell asleep (yes, God's word has done that for me as well). And I remember a passage of scripture from Psalm 4:4-5 NIV:

"*Tremble and do not sin;*

When you are on your beds,

Search your hearts and be silent. Offer the sacrifices of the righteous and trust in the Lord."

Then over and over I would repeat to myself, "Be still and know that God is God."

But Who was God though, really?

My soul needed a deeper knowledge and experience of The Lord God's presence to know and understand who He was so that I could finally learn to be still and rest.

I then learned 2 Peter 1:2: NASB

Grace and peace be multiplied to you in the knowledge of God and of Jesus our Lord...

That means I needed more time studying and taking *hold* of God's word, meditating and praying to know Him more and more each day. I desired eternal divorce from mental illness and sin and a deep intimacy with my Heavenly Father. That was a divine diamond that I ended up excavating from the Word of God. I now knew that I had to be inside the presence of God through Christ, meditating and believing on the faithfulness of the Father throughout the scriptures and imitating the ministry of and being transformed into the image of the Son. As I focus and move towards this calling from Jesus, into my soul is downloaded His grace and peace which is then multiplied by His peace and grace for the rest of my life and through eternity.

For He makes me lay down in green pastures and leads me beside still waters…The Lord has given only to Himself the authority to restore my soul. So given the state that I was in, I borrowed the request of David where he said that I desire only to then dwell in your house and mediate in your temple. I desired my soul to know God's stillness. For there is no peace for the wicked, nor is the blessing on the person who walks in the counsel of the wicked. For just as the blessing is on the person who takes delight in the meditation of the law of the Lord, Jesus said that every weary and burdened person who comes to the Him, the Word of God, will be given rest. That's a promise.

"*He lets me rest in green meadows; he leads me beside peaceful streams.*"

Psalm 23:2 NLT

…when the Lord becomes your Sheppard. He invites you to invite Him, but He doesn't force.

…*I will also give you rest from all your enemies…*

2 Samuel 7:11 NIV

…when your desire is for My heart, to dwell in My House, and for your heart to become My Temple.

> "Come to Me, all you who are weary and burdened, and I will give you rest." Matthew 11:28 NIV

…But only if you desire rest.

Man Shall Not Live On Bread…Alone

Now Ahab told Jezebel everything Elijah had done and how he had killed all the prophets with the sword. So Jezebel sent a messenger to Elijah to say, "May the gods deal with me, be it ever so severely, if by this time tomorrow I do not make your life like that of one of them."

Elijah was afraid and ran for his life. When he came to Beersheba in Judah, he left his servant there, while he himself went a day's journey into the wilderness. He came to a broom bush, sat down under it and prayed that he might die. "I have had enough, LORD," he said. "Take my life; I am no better than my ancestors." Then he lay down under the bush and fell asleep.

All at once an angel touched him and said, "Get up and eat." He looked around, and there by his head was some bread baked over hot coals, and a jar of water. He ate and drank and then lay down again.

The angel of the LORD came back a second time and touched him and said, "Get up and eat, for the journey is too much for you." So he got up and ate and drank. Strengthened by that food, he traveled forty days and forty nights until he reached Horeb, the mountain of God. 1 Kings 19:1-8 NIV

One of the first questions paramedics or anyone will ask when having an episode is, "Did you eat today?"

Our negative situations and experiences in life can be so stressful and burdensome, leading us to all kinds of paranoias, fears and thinking that is opposite to the renewed mindset of Jesus Christ. It is a spiritual work in progress. It takes godly patience, yet godly persistence, and faith in God's word to be built back up again. There was a period of time where

I was so afraid of dying and panic attacks, and having an episode I would call 911 for help on the fly. But once they got to my apartment, only to find out that nothing was wrong with my heart and I could breathe fine, they suspected something else was amiss. Yet when I continued to call them, they finally took me into the hospital facility and admitted me. My focus daily used to be paying close attention to my breathing constantly, wondering if I was having a heart attack after the complete numbing of my arms, and the feeling of being "choked". Where I was normally 180-190lbs, I stressed myself down to 150lbs. I then remember fighting back with God, taking every minute and chance I had to spend time with Him. Because every minute I wasn't thinking about Him was a minute dedicated to thinking about another panic attack and my other problems. I had my fears, insecurities, my sins and the fear of the consequences of them to work through with God. Fear of punishment and death can be so paralyzing when mixing itself with mental illness, snatching away my peace…as well as my appetite.

Elijah, in fear of death at the hands of Jezebel (because he killed 400 of her false prophets of Baal), ran so far away to where the Angel of the Lord had to tell him he needed to eat twice, "for the journey is too much for you."

When walking on this difficult journey, one thing is quite the given:

You must eat to keep moving towards healing because hunger and starving the body of vitamins and resources makes mental illness worse. Drink **MORE THAN** *plenty of water while you're at it too.*

Only One King And Priest

The Philistines assembled to fight Israel, with three thousand chariots, six thousand charioteers, and soldiers as numerous as the sand on the seashore. They went up and camped at MiKmash, east of Beth-Aven. When the Israelites saw that their situation was critical and that their army was hard pressed, they hid in caves and thickets, among the rocks, and in pits and cisterns. Some Hebrews even crossed the Jordan to the land of Gad and Gilead.

Saul remained at Gilgal, and all the troops with him were quaking with fear. He waited seven days, the time set by Samuel; but Samuel did not come to Gilgal, and Saul's men began to scatter. So he said, "Bring me the burnt offering and the fellowship offerings." And Saul offered up the burnt offering. Just as he finished making the offering, Samuel arrived, and Saul went out to greet him.

"What have you done?" asked Samuel. Saul replied, "When I saw that the men were scattering, and that you did not come at the set time, and that the Philistines were assembling at Mikmash, I thought, 'Now the Philistines will come down against me at Gilgal, and I have not sought the Lord's favor.' So I felt compelled to offer the burnt offering."

"You have done a foolish thing," Samuel said. "You have not kept the command the Lord your God gave you; if you had, he would have established your kingdom over Israel for all time. But now your kingdom will not endure; the Lord has sought out a man after his own heart and appointed him ruler of his people, because you have not kept the Lord's command." 1 Samuel 13:5-14 NIV

The result:

Now the Spirit of the Lord had departed from Saul, and an evil spirit from the Lord tormented him. 1 Samuel 16:14 NIV

Mental illness and distress can derive from the decisions that we've made in our own lives. There are some main points that we going to discuss in this chapter regarding this.

1. A lack of patience can hinder or even cancel your future prosperity, blessings and promises.

Because of Saul's disobedience, the entire lineage of kings that were scheduled to reign in Israel after him was canceled by God and their future kingships was revoked. We all have done things out of fear or pride that we now wish we could turn back the hands of time to change the course of our life. We all have had feelings that this is the last chance will have to do this or that or I'm going to miss out. Making decisions to move ahead of God can cause a long season in your life experiencing pain, if it's not fatal. The feeling that if we don't do this here right now at this moment that it is going to cost us dearly. But God said to wait for Him so that our strength would be renewed. So we can see that when God commands us to wait for Him, it's not because God needs to stop and tie his shoe or that He's sluggish and having a lazy morning. It's because any decision we make outside of His leading, provision and instruction is a decision made out of our weakness and can make us even more vulnerable to repercussions both physical and spiritual.

2. A delay in obedience to God will indeed cause you hardship, because it is still disobedience and thus sin.

One of the major regrets I have in life is that I did not seek and listen to God sooner. Not because of the hardship and trials I experienced, but because of how amazing it is to be at peace with my soul because I finally decided to make peace with God through Christ Jesus. I do understand that our experience makes us who we are, but like Adam and Eve before the Fall, godly ignorance is a valuable treasure for the conscience and mental focus. It took me 20+ years of being distracted by the pleasures of my flesh, wasting time, stagnancy, and spinning my wheels to discover who Terrence was and why he existed. The problem was that I was too busy ducking, dodging and running from the only one who had the answer. Here I was running from God like an idiot (and I'm speaking for myself) when He was trying to forgive me, love me and give me a greater purpose for living. I was foolishly convinced that He wanted to punishment me. I would later discover, even as I'm now writing this, it wasn't even me running from God, it was the sin and guilt that I was controlled by and chained to dragging me away from their judgment. Not my own judgment! I'm created in God's image, not the sin and guilt. This is why we are considered to be like sheep because our only true self-defense mechanism is to cry out loud and say, "Father, the enemy is trying to kill me! Abba Father, help!

3. Stay in your lane…

Or else you'll end up driving off of a cliff. There's only one God and Savior. There's only one qualified to carry out the duties of both King and Priest; that is the man Christ Jesus. Notice that King Saul's actions to make a sacrifice were motivated by the peer pressures of the people he was supposed to be king over. Don't let anyone's actions and emotions influence you to make a decision or decisions that are in opposition to God's commands and instructions. Peer pressures of conforming to "the norm", wanting to be accepted by everyone and fit in with the crowd, or maybe it's a boy or a girl you want to like you. And this person or people are enticing you to do some things that you know violates your integrity and you know it's not right or wouldn't sit well with wise authority. These things sometimes have caused us to step outside of ourselves and who we are called to be only to entrap ourselves into things that are even now difficult for us to get out of or away from. In Saul's case, there was only one king and priest who is called to rule and be a sacrifice simultaneously. That is man Christ Jesus. Yet, in King Saul's day, the priest Samuel was to fulfill the *sacrificing* role to the Lord. Saul stepped out of his boundaries due to his impatience, blaming the influence of the people and due to his disobedience to God. So in turn, God released him and his future lineage from the kingship. For the sake of good will in your life, don't get out of character trying to fit in with everyone or being influenced by everyone and everything around you. Stay inside of your zone and be patient. In this way you won't be refused the promises of God due to your own doing. When we move ahead to God, we, out of ignorance and impatience, run ahead of God or even attempt to take the throne of God. In this case, we foolishly invite Christ into *our* "will" instead of operating in *His* will. The end result is that we end up in a ditch that we are now trying to dig out of; such as an addiction or unhealthy and dangerous relationship. *"How did I end up here? How did I allow things to go this far?"* you'll ask. Do not be in this position. Resorting to alcohol, drugs or stepping outside of our marriages will lead us into even greater detriment. And once the enemy has his hook in your mind and in your heart he'll move to disassemble and devour you in order to subdue you to destruction.

Three Strand Cord

Two are better than one because they have a good reward for their labor. For if they fall, one will lift up his companion. But woe to him who is alone when he falls, For he has no one to help him up. Again, if two lie down together, they will keep warm; But how can one be warm alone? Though one may be overpowered by another, two can withstand him. And a threefold cord is not quickly broken.

Ecclesiastes 4: 9 – 12 NKJV

One of the things that I know I would not want anyone to experience is going through mental illness alone. Unfortunately, I didn't like to talk about my mental illness for fear of being written off as someone who might be too unstable or needy to be around. Another fear of mines was being considered "crazy" and a "yellow light signal." I felt that the feelings and emotions that were real to me would be obscure and strange to someone else that may be oblivious to what it feels like to go through mental illness, so I dealt with it alone. But I remember one day some of my friends and I from my old job, we all planned a little day trip to Universal City Walk in Los Angeles in 2011. We barely spent any money or did anything what could be considered "spectacular", we were just enjoying the beautiful day. We all had the day off....Anyways, I knew that I was going through something but when I was with them I felt "upheld" and secure. My mind was focused on enjoying my day and continuing to live life. Even though they may not have known the extent of what I was going through, they were there. I was not alone. It was blessing from God and He used them to bless me without them even knowing it. Another time, I think in 2012 we planned a trip to San Diego, CA during the weekday. Once again, we had the day off….We coasted down the 5 freeway and saw the horizon where the sky met the Pacific Ocean. San Diego, by the way is a chill city and me being from the laid back Midwest, I felt like it was my pace of life at the time. I believe having godly humility, transparency and the willingness to be vulnerable would have opened the doors for God to bless me in my season of illness and sped up my healing much faster. I possibly missed several opportunities to be a blessing, encouragement and comfort to others. But I kept quiet about it for the most part. I was tempted to believe that I wasn't ready to share and believed the fear of rejection. Another part of me felt I needed to be healed before I could say anything. Lord forgive me for those thoughts if they were wrong. I felt I needed to find my way through mental illness first then show others the Way to Christ through Christ. I allowed the enemy to blind me to the truth that there are so many other people in my family, community, the country, the entire world experiencing what Christ delivered me from. Nonetheless, God remains good, He remains faithful. I now see that after the Lord God led me through, He placed me above the valley of the shadow of death. I believe that it was so I could now shout back through to the exit and declare and proclaim with a loud voice above that same valley where the Lord Jesus fixed me, "Victory is here! Keep pressing through towards and in Christ Jesus! He delivered me from the valley! Follow HIM, keep moving, and keep going!!" Letting someone who you can talk to know that you are going through a difficult season in life sometimes gives others the opportunity and the blessing from God to help us carry our burdens. But we MUST say something. Christ Jesus cares for us. He will help us through anything. The point I'm making is this: We weren't made to go through the troubles of life alone. Yes, we must be responsible for our healing and growth, and use wisdom and discernment concerning what we share, the appropriate time to share, and whom to share with. Yet at the end of it all we need help to live life. We need the shoulders, love, correction, teaching, rebuke and encouragement of others to grow.

"Abide in Me, and I in you. As the branch cannot bear fruit of itself unless it abides in the vine, so neither can you unless you abide in Me. "I am the vine, you are the branches; he who abides in Me and I in him, he bears much fruit, for apart from Me you can do nothing. "If anyone does not abide in Me, he is thrown away as a branch and dries up; and they gather them, and cast them into the fire and they are burned.

John 15:4-6 NKJV

We are stronger and alive in Christ (and with His body – the church). Through Christ Jesus, we are mightier together than apart from each other.

And forgive Us Our Debts

Our debts to God are our trespasses. In other words, they are the sins we have committed in life that will in the end separate us from God forever. Only the sacrifice of Jesus Christ could have paid the price our souls would have had to pay without Him. And that price would not get us into heaven but it would be an eternal separation from God and the fires of hell forever and ever. And in order to escape the lake of financial Gehenna, that's exactly how we need to view financial debt: a sin - one that separates us from the godly peace we desire in life. In Proverbs, Solomon warns us never to be surety for a friend. Never sign your name in this manner (unless they are your child or spouse, and even that's risky) under someone else's ambitions, wants and desires that will eventually drag you into financial ruin with them. And most of the time, that ambition is coming from that very nice, friendly and well-put together representative of a credit card company offering you their "low monthly payment" credit card. Well, the bible says that Lucifer was actually attractive and the most beautiful of all the angels created by God - and the best credit card you can sign up for in life is the "no monthly payment-ever" credit card.

Just like Jesus said that no one goes into hell blindfolded, no one goes into financial ruin blindfolded either.

Utterly shutdown and cut up just about any credit card offer and surety - with a chainsaw. When it comes to this vice of debt and surety, you will want to apply overkill. Credit cards and surety do the exact same thing to us that sin does - it lies to us with the temptation of instant gratification and pleasure then when we are hooked, it chains itself to us and it drags us into financial destruction.

Other "DDAD's" (Debts Disguised As Deals) you may want to shut down immediately or use extreme wisdom and discernment when using them. These are the "there will never be another deal like this again" deals, or the "you just can't beat it" deals. There are a couple of DDAD's that introduce themselves by playing on your heartstrings and they are usually initiated by family (not necessarily loved ones) and friends such as the "I'll help you pay it back, I promise" deals or the "you can pay that off in no time!" deals. It's funny how these characters are experts in knowing what you can do with your money. There are some that may rock the boat a bit with the, "You should do it because I'm your wife or I'm your husband" deals or "if you loved me you would do it" deals, maybe the "I would do it for you!" deals. I love and thank my mother dearly for sowing in me this kind of attitude towards financial debt. When I was younger, I gave her a lot of push back for not giving me a credit card. When she saw that I came home for semester break during my first year of college with a new t-shirt she asked me, "Where did you get that T-shirt from, the one you're wearing?? I responded, "Oh, oh, I got this from school. They were handing them out and all you had to do is fill out a form..." So when the credit card came in the mail, she said, "Terrence, come here. Your credit card came in the mail." So like a sloth, made my way on over to her, then she said, "Take a good look at this card, because this is the last time you're going to see it!" She then grabbed the near-by scissors and cut the credit card into small pieces. She taught me over time through her own experience to ruin the credit card's life before the credit card ruin mines! If you want to talk about having peace and rest with minimized distress and anxiety in your life, then start seeing debt as a sin and disease. You must to come to a place in your life where you literally hate owing debt. Seek help to take an aggressive approach to eliminate debt in your life forever as well as seeking Christ and counselors to help you eliminate the root causes of debt-causing habits. Because debt isn't a *responsibility*, they are, in every way, more so a *liability and threat*. I reiterate: Do not, if applicable, under no circumstances draw near to using credit cards and surety because they will ruin your life.

Building Altars

Everywhere you turn, everything you see in your atmosphere and everything in your life should be an altar dedicated to the Lord. There must be surrounding pillars and altars in your daily coming out and going in that continuously bring you into the presence and sanctuary of God. The goal is to exchange your worldly atmosphere for the glory and nearness of God and Heaven over and in your life.

Genesis chapters 12 and 13 talk about the altars of God that Abram (Abraham) built in each land the Lord God led Him to.

The altars were these:

1. An altar to commemorate God's faithfulness and fellowship – Abram and all that He owned arrived to the land that God had promised him. Then God visited Abram after he arrived to Canaan to show him that He is the God who keeps His promises.

2. An altar of praise and intimacy –

This is the altar where Abram worshipped the Lord God. It was in the hill country between Bethel and Ai so it was in a higher place. It also says in Genesis 12:8 NKJV, that after the visiting of the Lord when arriving to Canaan, Abram then traveled southward and set up camp. So not only did Abram go higher, he stepped into the promises of God by going deeper and deeper. Yet when the famine came in the land, Abram left the altar of

God behind and headed for Egypt for safety. This is what happens when we decide to go higher by going deeper in the Lord, and deeper by reaching higher to God. When the trials come, our first inclination is to flee or take back the wheel from God. But the altar of God stands strong forever. Abram failed to remember the Lord God in whom he first trusted and instead placed his trust to be saved from the famine in Pharaoh. Difficult seasons in life, I tell you, are able to become an agent in us becoming distracted from continuously seeking, serving and staying in fellowship with God. When arriving to Egypt, Abram feared that Pharaoh would take his life and take Sarai for himself, seeing that she was very beautiful. So, in efforts to save himself, Abram's plan was to act as if Sarai was his sister instead of his wife and trade her in to Pharaoh, because if they found out that Sarai was his wife, Abram feared they would kill him. But God sent a plague on the land because of Sarai, and Abram and Sarai were removed from the land of Egypt, forcing them to return to the altar of God that Abram built in the hills of the land promised. It was still standing there. Abram returned to God's altar and again worshipped Him.

3. An altar of Abram taking hold of the Promise –

In every direction and as far as Abram could see, God said to explore the land because He was going to fill all of it through him. The music you play in your home needs to go from the secular to songs of worship and praise to the Lord. The work or job you do must be unto the Lord. The time given towards serving others or your leisure time must be dedicated to the worship of God and Sabbath with God. When I began creating art and accepted the truth that the Lord gave me a creative mind, I asked God, "What should I create?" The Holy Spirit said, "Create the Word of God." Then He blessed me to "see" and artistically create the scriptures in symbolic form so that when I create, like young Samuel in the temple of the Lord, I too could minister to the Lord; by His Word and a paint brush. The music I created exuded from the presence of His glory in Christ surrounding me and Eternal Life alive inside of me. The biblical paintings I created were fixed on the walls of my home to the point that when I walked inside from the world, I'd walk into the house of God.

Unless I was watching a documentary about Jesus, art or God's creation, my television stayed off.

I had 24-hour access to the internet through my phone and computer and this 24-hour access was strictly used (and still is) for the consistent hearing of the Gospel. I remained saturated with the Word of God. All I did was go to a website that plays videos, I typed in the subject or concern that was on my heart, then type either the word "bible or gospel" after the subject I was looking for. I then scrolled to find the subject that the Holy Spirit had spoken to me and then selected my pastor or teacher for the day. It was like a vending machine from the Kingdom of Heaven. The best thing is that second's, third's, fourth's, all the way up to until I fell asleep if I wanted were free. After the message from my first pastor had concluded, I could come back later on and make another selection and repeat the process over and over for 24 hours, 7 days a week. I do have a home church to where I attend and pay my tithes. But outside of my church, I've adopted about 7 or 8 pastors through the World Wide Web. I'm going to use a little slang here: I stay "fill't" with God's word. While driving in my car, somebody is either preaching the Gospel of Jesus or singing the worship of Jesus to me on the radio. Otherwise, my radio stays off. When I go to the park or to the beach I sit and I thank God for allowing me to see and hear the beauty of His creation. If not that, I'm there, just Him and I, sharing the weights of my heart with my Heavenly Father. Whether the former or latter, I need for God through Christ to have full and complete access to all of me. For He is the only One who can do anything about everything concerning me. Sometimes pillars and altars to God aren't in a physical space but rather a specific time of day. I was having a conversation with an older man of God who is also a judge. We were talking and he shared with me that he wakes up at 4 a.m. every morning to seek God in His word, prays through the inspiration of the scriptures he heard and read, and after that he listens to worship music – all before he starts his morning run and work day. When someone shares with me the different ways they maintain their growth and relationship with God that I'm not doing, for me, I tend to take it as God letting me know through that person to *do this Terrence.* So one day I got up at about 4:30a.m. (don't judge me for being late) to seek God in His word and I can't explain or articulate how quiet the house and the neighborhood around me was. The ability to hear clearly the heart of God through the scriptures as I'm reading them, and then having the time in the morning to meditate on His word and instruction without feeling rushed or distracted is priceless. On a different morning, as I was reading and meditating on the scriptures, the understanding and its practical application came to my heart and mind. After that, the inspiration of the Holy Spirit led me to minister back to God which initiated a back and forth dialogue on what I was learning from Him. The study came from Psalms 34: 8-11 NASB. I ended up having the desire to minister to my wife an then she was blessed by God's word in the morning. God showed me that altars to Him must be built in my marriage and in my relationship with my children. As I'm thinking about this truth, I'm asking God, "Where else in addition to ministering to my wife do I need to build altars to You, Father in my marriage and my role as a husband?" For marriage must honor God, because He instituted it. But if I did not obey God's call to wake up, grab my bible and build His altar then my wife and I would have missed the opportunity to be fed, fellowship, and be blessed by the Lord at the start of the day. I would have missed the opportunity to realize that I must build altars in my relationship with my family and friends. Everything we do and say to each other must honor and give glory to Him. My goal in life is this: to dwell in the house of the Lord all the days of my life and to meditate day and night on Him in His temple. That's how I was rescued from mental oppression. This is how the walls of Jericho in my life were broken down in front of me: by placing in my life, my Heavenly Father first and before me. And when God stands before me, then He stands face to face in front of Satan and his tactics. Psalm 23:5 BSB says, "You prepare a table before me in the presence of my enemies. You anoint my head with oil; my cup overflows" God knows I love chicken Alfredo, steamed veggies, sweet potatoes with a little butter and cinnamon, sometimes a little "Surf and Turf" for the times I'm feeling a little "fancy" and always to top it off – dark chocolate cake. The Lord prepared my meal and supplications in front of the devil's face and then told me to sit back and enjoy the show. The movie I'm watching was called "My Daddy is Here." And as long as I stay at God's dinner table, as long as I stay spiritually full on God's Word, then the movie never stops. And when Jesus Christ came to "this Earth", to this body made from the dust, and came into my heart, God gave me His everlasting covenant and He stood up as my defense as my shield and as my fortress. As I began to declare the Word of God aloud and meditate on His promises and began to shout His praise around the situations in my life, demons began to tremble and flee because the walls started crumbling down until the scorpions and serpents laid crushed beneath my feet through the power of God's Holy Spirit. This is the authority of Christ Jesus: If He is standing with me, none can stand against me. For every knee shall bow and every tongue must confess that Jesus Christ is Lord of all. Amen

What Say You? Answering Pride

'This is what it means, O' King. This is what the Most High said would happen to my lord the king: You will be driven away from all people and will live with the wild animals of the field. You will eat grass like cattle and become wet with the water from heaven. Seven years will pass until you understand that the Most High is ruler over the nations of men, and gives them to whomever He wants. It was said that the base of the tree and its roots must be left. This means that your nation will be returned to you after you understand that it is Heaven that rules. So, O king, may my words be pleasing to you. Turn away from your sins by doing what is right and good. Turn away from your wrong-doing by being kind to the poor. Then it may be that things will keep going well for you.'

The King Loses It All

"All this happened to King Nebuchadnezzar. Twelve months later he was walking on the roof of his beautiful house in Babylon. And he said, 'Is not this the great Babylon which I have built as a beautiful place for the king? I have built it by my great strength and for the greatness of my power.' Before the king was finished speaking, a voice came from heaven, saying, 'King Nebuchadnezzar, to you it is said: Your power over the nation has been taken from you. You will be driven away from all people and will live with the wild animals of the field. You will eat grass like cattle. And seven years will pass until you understand that the Most High is ruler over the nations of men, and gives them to whomever He wants.' At once these words about Nebuchadnezzar came true. He was driven away from all people and began eating grass like cattle. His body became wet with the water from heaven, until his hair grew as long as eagles' feathers and his nails like those of birds.

Nebuchadnezzar Praises God

"But at the end of that time I, Nebuchadnezzar, looked up toward heaven and my understanding returned to me. And I gave thanks to the Most High and praised and honored Him Who lives forever. For His nation lasts forever, and His rule is for all people for all time. All the people of the earth are thought of as nothing. He does as He pleases with the angels of heaven and the people of the earth. No one can hold back His hand or say to Him, 'What have You done?' At that time my understanding returned to me. And my honor and power were returned to me for the greatness of my nation. My wise men and my leaders began looking for me, and I was made king again, with even more greatness added to me. Now I, Nebuchadnezzar, praise and honor the King of heaven. For all His works are true and His ways are right. And He is able to bring down those who walk in pride." My grandmother's presence in my life was a huge component towards being implanted with the seeds necessary to know God and to choose according to His word what's right from wrong. While growing up, I always remember her saying the phrase "A hard head makes a soft behind." My grandmother couldn't have preached harder to me, taken me to more Sunday church services, nor shared more bible scriptures with me. Whether she encouraged me with her loving peace towards Christ or a stern rebuke, I had a choice to either humble myself or not. And I foolishly chose to take the hard road unknowingly to salvation. I was a young man stuck in my ways wanting to do whatever I wanted to do in life but on someone else's dime. I was chained to a life of carousing, partying and "living my life" while being oblivious to the nudging of God's forgiveness and love and sometimes I feel I ignored Him. All my grandmother could do is pray for me after a while. In 2006, I ended up leaving Cleveland, Ohio to try my "luck" in Orange County, California. I ended up landing a summer internship that ended up becoming an over-a-decade-job. After a year or so, my past sins, the condemning thoughts as well as the convictions and call of God would finally catch up to me. By this time, the "high" of being able to say I lived in Southern California began to wear off. It's like both were running after me for their own purposes: Satan, to bring me to death while God, to bring His child to life through Christ. Just in case you didn't know, if there is one place a person can get "caught up and completely lost" and never return, it's SoCal. I remember the day that the Holy Spirit was nudging me towards the scriptures. I was at my condo in the Summer of 2007 or so and it was about two hours before it was time for me to go to work and it felt like something was "missing" in my spirit or I needed to do something. And when I sat down and opened the bible that was laying around the house and started reading it there was peace that fell over me. I didn't want to stop reading but I had to leave to be on time for work. The desire to read faded and was eventually snatched away without me recognizing that God was trying to speak to me concerning my deep need for Him and His word in my life. Whether by distractions or by my lack of wisdom in realizing that the bible was much more than a book to read, the enemy took advantage of that and once again I stopped reading. And then over a period of time things just started happening. About 2009, I had been out in Cali and at my job for three years and I had no clue as to who I was or what I was supposed to be doing. I felt as though I was just going through the motions in life as a hamster in a wheel. The stresses of life and still carrying on in sin in my body began to take a toll on me. I was filling myself with pornography once more, which lead to sexual immorality, which lead to fears of judgment by God and death. This moved me into having violent panic attacks and high anxiety that lead to hypertension and high blood pressure that reached levels of 150/90 at the age of 30. It kind of reminds me of how I think about Jonah was in the whale; my vision was pitch black with no light anywhere while at the mercy of the one or the thing guiding my atmosphere. The fears and the cries that were sent to God for His help weighed on Jonah's spirit to a breaking point: the place where God used to get Jonah to declare, "Yes, God, I will do whatever You say." No matter how much I tried to advance or succeed, if God did not approve then the whale didn't either. Then if I didn't have permission to move, then I had to just sit there until I did what Jonah did: humble myself or rather be humbled by God. And that was what mental illness was like for me. While battling mental illness, the same person that tried to speak to me and sow into me constantly about the love of God is the same person who would call me and read me bible scriptures and pray with me, praying for my break through: grandma. She finally had my attention because God had my attention. There was nothing else she could do. I had to finally make the decision for Jesus Christ for myself. I've heard a pastor say, "God is willing to put up with your captivity as long as you are, but as soon as you repent, the Father will run to you and throw His arms around you just like the child who was lost but now has been found." In my study of Daniel later on during my healing process, I came across the scripture where Nebuchadnezzar had a terrifying dream from God. After interpreting the dream, Daniel strongly advised Nebuchadnezzar to humble himself and turn to righteousness. Because Babylon had become so great, the king given the praise and credit of Babylon's success to himself opposed to the One who made him great: The Lord. Though Nebuchadnezzar knew that Daniel had the insight and interpretations of the Lord Most High, he still chose to praise himself for the success of Babylon instead of giving God the honor and glory. As soon as the words of pride left the king's mouth, he was judged to walk the face of the earth for seven years being given the mind of a beast, until, as the scriptures say, "You know and declare that the Most High reigns on heaven and earth." And the king wandered seven years…until he came to his senses and gave the Lord Most High praise as ruler of heaven and earth. From that point on Nebuchadnezzar's glory and right mind was returned to him.

What Then, Say You?

<u>Conquering Self – Worth</u>

And I am certain that God, who began the good work within you, will continue his work until it is finally finished on the day when Christ Jesus returns

Philippians 1:6 NLT

For you formed my inward parts; you knitted me together in my mother's womb. I praise you, for I am fearfully and wonderfully made. Wonderful are your works; my soul knows it very well. My frame was not hidden from you, when I was being made in secret, intricately woven in the depths of the earth.

Psalm 139:13-15 ESV

Are not five sparrows sold for two copper coins? And not one of them is forgotten before God. But the very hairs of your head are all numbered. Do not fear therefore; you are of more value than many sparrows.

Luke 12: 6 -7 NKJV

The LORD your God is in your midst, a victorious warrior. He will exult over you with joy, He will be quiet in His love, He will rejoice over you with shouts of joy.

Zephaniah 3:17 NASB

<u>Direction/Instruction/Relationships:</u>

Blessed is the one who does not walk in step with the wicked or stand in the way that sinners take or sit in the company of mockers, but whose delight is in the law of the Lord, and who meditates on his law day and night. That person is like a tree planted by streams of water, which yields its fruit in season and whose leaf does not wither — whatever they do prospers.

Psalm 1:1-3 NIVUK

I therefore, a prisoner for the Lord, urge you to walk in a manner worthy of the calling to which you have been called, with all humility and gentleness, with patience, bearing with one another in love, eager to maintain the unity of the Spirit in the bond of peace. There is one body and one Spirit—just as you were called to the one hope that belongs to your call— one Lord, one faith, one baptism,

Ephesians 4:1 ESV

Seek his will in all you do, and he will show you which path to take.

Proverbs 3:6 NLT

<u>Temptation</u>

No temptation has overtaken you that is not common to man. God is faithful, and he will not let you be tempted beyond your ability, but with the temptation he will also provide the way of escape, that you may be able to endure it.

1 Corinthians 10:13 ESV

When tempted, no one should say, "God is tempting me." For God cannot be tempted by evil, nor does He tempt anyone.

James 1:13 NIV

Fear/ Worry/ Depression

So do not fear, for I am with you; do not be dismayed, for I am your God. I will strengthen you and help you; I will uphold you with my righteous right hand

Isaiah 41:10 NIV

Needing Strength

I came to you in weakness—timid and trembling. And my message and my preaching were very plain. Rather than using clever and persuasive speeches, I relied only on the power of the Holy Spirit. I did this so you would trust not in human wisdom but in the power of God.

1 Corinthians 2:3-5 NLT

Then Jesus said, "Come to me, all of you who are weary and carry heavy burdens, and I will give you rest. Take my yoke upon you. Let me teach you, because I am humble and gentle at heart, and you will find rest for your souls. For my yoke is easy to bear, and the burden I give you is light."

Matthew 11: 28 NLT

But those who hope in the LORD will renew their strength. They will soar on wings like eagles; they will run and not grow weary, they will walk and not be faint.

Isaiah 40:31 NIV

Peace

Now may the Lord of peace himself give you peace at all times in every way. The Lord be with you all.

2 Thessalonians 3:16 ESV

I have said these things to you, that in me you may have peace. In the world you will have tribulation. But take heart; I have overcome the world.

John 16:33 ESV

You will keep him in perfect peace, whose mind is stayed on You, because he trusts in You. Trust in the Lord forever, For the Lord God is an everlasting Rock.

Isaiah 26: 3-4 ESV

Do not be anxious about anything, but in everything by prayer and supplication with thanksgiving let your requests be made known to God. And the peace of God, which surpasses all understanding, will guard your hearts and your minds in Christ Jesus –

Philippians 4:6,7 ESV

God-fidence (Confidence)

For the Lord will be your confidence and will keep your foot from being caught.

Proverbs 3:26 NASB

This is my command—be strong and courageous! Do not be afraid or discouraged. For the Lord, your God is with you wherever you go

Joshua 1:9 NLT

Forgiveness

The LORD will accomplish what concerns me; Your lovingkindness, O LORD, is everlasting; Do not forsake the works of Your hands.

Psalm 138:8 NASB

'The LORD is slow to anger and abundant in lovingkindness, forgiving iniquity and transgression; but He will by no means clear the guilty, visiting the iniquity of the fathers on the children to the third and the fourth generations.'

Numbers 14:18 NASB

"Two men went up into the temple to pray, one a Pharisee and the other a tax collector." The Pharisee stood and was praying this to himself: 'God, I thank You that I am not like other people: swindlers, unjust, adulterers, or even like this tax collector. 'I fast twice a week; I pay tithes of all that I get. "But the tax collector, standing some distance away, was even unwilling to lift up his eyes to heaven, but was beating his breast, saying, 'God, be merciful to me, the sinner!' "I tell you, this man went to his house justified rather than the other; for everyone who exalts himself will be humbled, but he who humbles himself will be exalted."

Luke 18:10-14 NASB

Whenever you stand praying, forgive, if you have anything against anyone, so that your Father who is in heaven will also forgive you your transgressions. But if you do not forgive, neither will your Father who is in heaven forgive your transgressions.

Mark 11:25-26 NASB

For You, Lord, are good, and ready to forgive, And abundant in lovingkindness to all who call upon You.

Psalm 86:5 NASB

CPSIA information can be obtained
at www.ICGtesting.com
Printed in the USA
BVHW082110040719
552613BV00002B/268/P